MASTERING YOUR MIND: A COMPREHENSIVE GUIDE TO OVERCOMING BORDERLINE PERSONALITY DISORDER WITH COGNITIVE BEHAVIORAL THERAPY

ALICE JENNIFER

Contents

Understanding Borderline Personality Disorder: Symptoms, Causes, and Challenges

Borderline Personality Disorder (BPD) is a complex mental health condition that can significantly impact an individual's life, relationships, and overall well-being. It is crucial to understand the signs, symptoms, causes, and challenges associated with BPD to effectively manage and treat the disorder. In this chapter, we will explore these aspects in detail, providing you with a comprehensive understanding of BPD and its implications.

Recognizing the signs and symptoms of BPD

BPD is characterized by a persistent pattern of instability in emotions, self-image, and interpersonal relationships. The signs and symptoms of BPD can vary from person to person, but there are some common patterns to look out for.

One of the most prominent symptoms of BPD is emotional instability. People with BPD often experience intense and rapidly changing emotions that can last from a few hours to several days. These emotions can range from extreme happiness and euphoria to severe sadness, anger, and despair. The emotional instability can be triggered by seemingly minor events or perceived rejections, making it difficult for individuals with BPD to maintain stable relationships and a consistent sense of self.

For example, Sarah, who has been diagnosed with BPD, may feel extremely happy and content when her partner shows her affection. However, if her partner is unable to respond to a text message promptly, Sarah may quickly spiral into feelings of abandonment, rage, and worthlessness. This emotional rollercoaster can be exhausting and confusing for both Sarah and her loved ones.

Another key symptom of BPD is a distorted sense of self. Individuals with BPD often struggle with their identity and may have difficulty maintaining a stable self-image. They may frequently change their goals, values, and even their appearance in an attempt to find a sense of self that feels authentic and consistent. This instability in self-image can lead to impulsive behaviors, such as sudden changes in careers, relationships, or living situations.

For instance, Michael, who lives with BPD, may have a hard time defining his long-term goals and values. He may pursue a career in medicine one month, only to decide that he wants to become an artist the next. This inconsistency in his sense of self can make it challenging for Michael to establish a fulfilling and stable life path.

Impulsivity is another common symptom of BPD. People with BPD may engage in risky or self-destructive behaviors without considering the consequences. These behaviors can include substance abuse, reckless driving, unsafe sexual practices, or excessive spending. Impulsivity in BPD is often a way to cope with intense emotions or to fill a perceived void in one's life.

An example of this could be Emily, who struggles with BPD and often finds herself using alcohol to numb her emotional pain. When she feels rejected or abandoned by a friend, she may impulsively drink to excess, leading to dangerous situations and further damaging her relationships.

Interpersonal difficulties are also a hallmark of BPD. Individuals with BPD may have a deep fear of abandonment and go to great lengths to avoid real or perceived rejection. They may experience intense and unstable relationships characterized by alternating between idealization and devaluation of their loved ones. This "black and white" thinking can lead to frequent arguments, breakups, and reconciliations, creating a cycle of unstable and tumultuous relationships.

For example, when David starts a new romantic relationship, he may initially idealize his partner, believing they are perfect and can do no wrong. However, as soon as his partner shows any sign of imperfection or disagreement, David may quickly shift to devaluing them, feeling intense anger and disappointment. This pattern of idealization and devaluation can make it difficult for David to maintain long-lasting, healthy relationships.

It is important to note that not everyone with BPD will experience all of these symptoms, and the severity can vary from person to person. However, recognizing these signs and symptoms is crucial for seeking appropriate help and support.

Exploring the potential causes and risk factors

The exact causes of BPD are not fully understood, but research suggests that a combination of genetic, environmental, and neurological factors may contribute to the development of the disorder.

Studies have shown that there is a genetic component to BPD. Individuals with a family history of BPD or other mental health disorders, such as depression or substance abuse, are at a higher risk of developing the condition. While having a genetic predisposition does not guarantee that a person will develop BPD, it does increase their vulnerability.

Environmental factors, particularly childhood experiences, also play a significant role in the development of BPD. Traumatic events, such as physical, emotional, or sexual abuse, neglect, or abandonment, can significantly impact a child's emotional development and increase the risk of developing BPD. However, it is important to note that not everyone who experiences childhood trauma will develop BPD, and not everyone with BPD has a history of trauma.

For example, Olivia grew up in a household where she experienced emotional neglect and witnessed domestic violence between her parents. As a result, she struggled to form secure attachments and developed a fear of abandonment. These experiences may have contributed to her later diagnosis of BPD.

Neurological factors may also contribute to the development of

BPD. Research has shown that individuals with BPD may have differences in brain structure and function, particularly in areas related to emotion regulation and impulse control. These neurological differences may make it more difficult for people with BPD to manage their emotions and behaviors effectively.

It is essential to understand that no single factor causes BPD, and the disorder likely results from a complex interplay of genetic, environmental, and neurological factors. By recognizing these potential causes and risk factors, we can work towards developing targeted prevention and intervention strategies to support individuals who may be vulnerable to developing BPD.

Addressing common misconceptions about BPD

Despite increased awareness and understanding of mental health disorders, there are still many misconceptions surrounding BPD. These misconceptions can lead to stigma, discrimination, and barriers to treatment for those living with the disorder. In this section, we will address some of the most common misconceptions about BPD.

One prevalent misconception is that BPD is untreatable. This belief can lead to a sense of hopelessness for those diagnosed with the disorder and may discourage them from seeking help. However, this is far from the truth. While BPD can be challenging to treat, there are evidence-based therapies, such as Dialectical Behavior Therapy (DBT) and Mentalization-Based Treatment (MBT), that have been shown to be effective in managing symptoms and improving quality of life for individuals with BPD.

For example, Sophia was initially hesitant to seek treatment for her BPD, believing that there was no hope for improvement. However, after engaging in DBT, she learned valuable skills for regulating her emotions, tolerating distress, and communicating effectively. With consistent practice and support, Sophia was able to manage her symptoms and lead a more fulfilling life.

Another misconception is that people with BPD are manipulative or attention-seeking. This belief stems from a misunderstanding of the symptoms of BPD, particularly the intense fear of abandonment and the desperate attempts to avoid it. When viewed through this lens, behaviors that may seem manipulative are often a result of deep emotional pain and a lack of effective coping strategies.

It is crucial to approach individuals with BPD with empathy and understanding, recognizing that their behaviors are a reflection of their struggles, rather than a deliberate attempt to manipulate others. By providing compassionate support and teaching healthy coping mechanisms, we can help those with BPD learn to manage their emotions and build more stable relationships.

A third misconception is that BPD only affects women. While it is true that BPD is more commonly diagnosed in women, research suggests that men may be underdiagnosed due to differences in symptom presentation and societal expectations. Men with BPD may be more likely to exhibit symptoms such as anger outbursts, substance abuse, and risk-taking behaviors, which may be misattributed to other mental health disorders or viewed as "typical" male behavior.

For example, Robert had been struggling with intense emotions, impulsivity, and unstable relationships for years, but his symptoms were often dismissed as "anger issues" or "commitment phobia." It wasn't until he sought help from a mental health professional who recognized the signs of BPD that he was able to receive an accurate diagnosis and appropriate treatment.

Recognizing that BPD can affect individuals of all genders is essential for ensuring that everyone who needs help can access appropriate resources and support.

By addressing these common misconceptions about BPD, we can work towards reducing stigma, increasing understanding, and promoting access to effective treatment for those living with the disorder.

In conclusion, understanding the symptoms, causes, and challenges associated with BPD is crucial for providing effective support and treatment for individuals living with the disorder. Recognizing the signs and symptoms, such as emotional instability, distorted sense of self, impulsivity, and interpersonal difficulties, can help individuals and their loved ones seek appropriate help.

Exploring the potential causes and risk factors, including genetic predisposition, childhood experiences, and neurological factors, can help us develop targeted prevention and intervention strategies. Addressing common misconceptions, such as the belief that BPD is untreatable, that people with BPD are manipulative, or that it only affects women, is essential for reducing stigma and promoting access to care.

By increasing our understanding and awareness of BPD, we can foster a more compassionate and supportive environment for those living with the disorder. With the right treatment, support, and self-understanding, individuals with BPD can learn to manage their symptoms, build healthier relationships, and lead fulfilling lives.

2

Introduction to Cognitive Behavioral Therapy: How CBT Can Help Manage BPD

Cognitive Behavioral Therapy (CBT) is a widely used and highly effective form of psychotherapy that can be particularly helpful for individuals living with Borderline Personality Disorder (BPD). In this chapter, we will explore the principles and goals of CBT, examine how it can address specific challenges related to BPD, and discuss the importance of setting realistic expectations for treatment.

Understanding the principles and goals of CBT

CBT is based on the idea that our thoughts, feelings, and behaviors are interconnected and influence one another. The primary goal of CBT is to help individuals identify and change dysfunctional or distorted thoughts and beliefs that contribute to emotional distress and maladaptive behaviors.

The core principles of CBT include:

1. Thoughts influence emotions and behaviors: CBT emphasizes the powerful role that thoughts play in shaping our emotional experiences and behavioral responses. By identifying and modifying unhelpful thought patterns, individuals can improve their emotional well-being and make positive changes in their lives.

2. Collaborative approach: CBT is a collaborative process between the therapist and the client. The therapist works with the

client to identify treatment goals, develop strategies for change, and monitor progress. This collaborative approach empowers clients to take an active role in their own recovery and builds a sense of self-efficacy.

3. Present-focused: While CBT acknowledges the importance of past experiences in shaping current thoughts and behaviors, it primarily focuses on addressing current challenges and developing practical skills for managing distress in the present moment.

4. Skills-based: CBT is a skills-based approach that teaches individuals specific techniques and strategies for managing their thoughts, emotions, and behaviors. These skills can be practiced and applied in real-life situations, promoting lasting change and resilience.

The goals of CBT in treating BPD may include:

1. Reducing emotional instability: CBT can help individuals with BPD learn to identify and regulate their intense emotions, reducing the frequency and severity of emotional outbursts and mood swings.

2. Improving interpersonal relationships: By addressing dysfunctional thought patterns and behaviors that contribute to relationship difficulties, CBT can help individuals with BPD develop healthier, more stable relationships.

3. Enhancing self-esteem and sense of self: CBT can help individuals with BPD challenge negative beliefs about themselves and develop a more balanced and compassionate self-image.

4. Reducing impulsivity and self-destructive behaviors: Through the development of coping skills and problem-solving strategies, CBT can help individuals with BPD manage impulsive urges and reduce engagement in self-destructive behaviors.

By understanding the principles and goals of CBT, individuals with BPD can gain insight into how this therapeutic approach can help them manage their symptoms and improve their overall quality of life.

Examining how CBT can address specific challenges related to BPD

CBT is particularly well-suited to address the specific challenges faced by individuals with BPD. By targeting the thoughts, emotions, and behaviors that contribute to BPD symptoms, CBT can help individuals develop more adaptive coping strategies and improve their overall functioning.

One of the primary challenges associated with BPD is emotional dysregulation. Individuals with BPD often experience intense and rapidly shifting emotions that can be difficult to manage. CBT can help address this challenge by teaching emotion regulation skills, such as:

1. Mindfulness: Mindfulness involves paying attention to the present moment without judgment. By practicing mindfulness, individuals with BPD can learn to observe their emotions without getting caught up in them, reducing the intensity and duration of emotional outbursts.

Example: Sarah, who struggles with BPD, learns to practice mindfulness during her CBT sessions. When she notices herself starting to feel overwhelmed with anger, she takes a moment to focus on her breath and observe her thoughts and feelings without reacting to them. This helps her manage her anger more effectively and prevents her from engaging in impulsive behaviors.

2. Distress tolerance: Distress tolerance skills help individuals cope with intense emotions without resorting to maladaptive behaviors. CBT teaches techniques such as distraction, self-soothing, and acceptance to help individuals ride out emotional storms.

Example: Michael, who has BPD, often experiences intense feelings of emptiness and loneliness. Through CBT, he learns distress tolerance skills, such as engaging in a favorite hobby or calling a supportive friend, to help him manage these emotions without turning to substance abuse or other self-destructive behaviors.

Another challenge faced by individuals with BPD is interpersonal difficulties. CBT can help address this challenge by teaching effective communication and problem-solving skills, such as:

1. Assertiveness: Assertiveness involves expressing one's needs and boundaries clearly and respectfully. By learning to communicate assertively, individuals with BPD can improve their relationships and reduce conflict.

Example: Emily, who struggles with BPD, often has difficulty saying "no" to others, leading to feelings of resentment and anger. Through CBT, she learns assertiveness skills, such as using "I" statements and setting clear boundaries. This helps her navigate relationships more effectively and reduces the frequency of interpersonal conflicts.

2. Conflict resolution: CBT teaches problem-solving strategies that can help individuals with BPD address interpersonal conflicts in a healthy and productive manner. By learning to identify the root cause of conflicts and generate alternative solutions, individuals can improve their relationships and reduce the intensity of emotional outbursts.

Example: David, who has BPD, often gets into arguments with his partner over minor disagreements. Through CBT, he learns conflict resolution skills, such as active listening and compromise. By applying these skills, he is able to navigate disagreements more calmly and maintain a more stable relationship.

CBT can also help individuals with BPD address challenges related to self-image and identity. By identifying and challenging negative beliefs about oneself, CBT can help foster a more balanced and compassionate self-image. This may involve:

1. Cognitive restructuring: Cognitive restructuring involves identifying and modifying distorted or unhelpful thoughts. By learning to recognize and challenge negative beliefs about oneself, individuals with BPD can develop a more accurate and compassionate self-image.

Example: Olivia, who struggles with BPD, often has thoughts such as "I'm unlovable" or "I'm a failure." Through CBT, she learns to identify these thoughts as distortions and challenge them with evidence. By developing a more balanced perspective, she begins to see herself in a more positive light and experiences improvements in her self-esteem.

2. Positive self-talk: CBT encourages individuals to engage in positive self-talk and self-affirmations. By regularly practicing kind and supportive self-talk, individuals with BPD can foster a more compassionate and stable sense of self.

Example: Robert, who has BPD, often engages in harsh self-criticism. Through CBT, he learns to replace negative self-talk with more compassionate and encouraging statements, such as "I am doing my best" or "I am worthy of love and respect." By consistently practicing positive self-talk, he experiences improvements in his self-esteem and overall well-being.

By addressing these specific challenges related to emotional dysregulation, interpersonal difficulties, and self-image, CBT can provide individuals with BPD with the tools and strategies needed to manage their symptoms and improve their overall functioning.

Setting realistic expectations for treatment

When embarking on a journey of treatment with CBT for BPD, it is essential to set realistic expectations. While CBT can be highly effective in managing BPD symptoms, it is not a quick fix or a cure-all. Understanding what to expect from treatment can help individuals stay motivated, committed, and prepared for the challenges and successes along the way.

One important aspect of setting realistic expectations is understanding that progress takes time. BPD is a complex disorder that develops over many years, often rooted in early life experiences and deeply ingrained patterns of thinking and behaving. As such, it is unrealistic to expect overnight changes or immediate relief from all symptoms. CBT is a gradual process that requires consistent effort and practice to yield lasting results.

Example: Sophia, who has recently been diagnosed with BPD, starts CBT with the expectation that she will feel better after just a few sessions. When she still experiences emotional outbursts and relationship difficulties after a month of therapy, she becomes discouraged and considers giving up. Her therapist helps her understand that progress takes time and encourages her to celebrate small victories along the way, such as using a coping skill to manage an intense emotion or having a successful interpersonal interaction.

Another realistic expectation is that there may be setbacks and challenges along the way. While CBT provides individuals with valuable tools and strategies for managing BPD symptoms, it is normal to experience ups and downs in the recovery process.

Stressful life events, interpersonal conflicts, or other triggers may lead to a resurgence of symptoms or a temporary setback. It is important to view these challenges as opportunities for growth and learning rather than failures.

Example: Michael, who has been participating in CBT for several months, experiences a significant setback when he loses his job. He finds himself struggling with intense emotions and urges to engage in self-destructive behaviors. Rather than viewing this as a failure of treatment, he reaches out to his therapist for support and guidance. Together, they work on applying the skills he has learned to navigate this difficult situation and maintain his progress.

It is also important to have realistic expectations about the level of effort and commitment required for successful treatment. CBT is an active and collaborative process that requires individuals to take an active role in their own recovery. This may involve completing homework assignments, practicing skills outside of therapy sessions, and being willing to confront challenging thoughts and emotions. While the therapist provides guidance and support, ultimately, the individual is responsible for putting in the work necessary for change.

Example: Emily, who struggles with BPD, initially expects her therapist to "fix" her problems without much effort on her part. However, as she engages in CBT, she learns that her active participation is crucial for progress. She commits to completing her therapy homework, practicing her skills regularly, and being open and honest with her therapist about her struggles and successes. As a result, she begins to see meaningful improvements in her symptoms and overall well-being.

Finally, it is essential to have realistic expectations about the outcome of treatment. While CBT can lead to significant improvements in BPD symptoms and overall functioning, it may not eliminate all challenges or guarantee a life free from emotional distress. The goal of CBT is to provide individuals with the tools and strategies needed to manage their symptoms effectively, build resilience, and lead a more fulfilling life, even in the face of ongoing challenges.

Example: David, who has completed a course of CBT for BPD, has made significant progress in managing his emotions and improving his relationships. However, he still experiences occasional mood swings and interpersonal conflicts. Rather than viewing this as a failure of treatment, he recognizes that these challenges are a normal part of life and that he now has the skills and resources to navigate them more effectively. He continues to practice his CBT skills and seek support when needed, maintaining his progress and resilience over time.

In conclusion, CBT is a highly effective treatment approach for managing the symptoms and challenges associated with BPD. By understanding the principles and goals of CBT, examining how it can address specific challenges related to BPD, and setting realistic expectations for treatment, individuals with BPD can embark on a journey of recovery and personal growth.

Through the collaborative and skills-based approach of CBT, individuals can learn to regulate their emotions, improve their interpersonal relationships, enhance their self-esteem, and reduce impulsivity and self-destructive behaviors. While progress may take time and require consistent effort, the tools and strategies gained through CBT can lead to lasting improvements in overall functioning and quality of life.

By setting realistic expectations and understanding that setbacks and challenges are a normal part of the recovery process, individuals can maintain motivation and commitment to treatment. With the guidance and support of a skilled therapist, individuals with BPD can develop the resilience and coping skills needed to navigate life's challenges and build a more fulfilling and satisfying life.

3

Identifying and Challenging Dysfunctional Thoughts: Techniques for Cognitive Restructuring

In the previous chapter, we explored the principles and goals of Cognitive Behavioral Therapy (CBT) and how it can help manage the symptoms and challenges associated with Borderline Personality Disorder (BPD). A key component of CBT is cognitive restructuring, which involves identifying and modifying dysfunctional or distorted thoughts that contribute to emotional distress and maladaptive behaviors. In this chapter, we will delve deeper into the process of cognitive restructuring, focusing on recognizing negative thought patterns, learning techniques to challenge and reframe dysfunctional thoughts, and practicing self-compassion and positive self-talk.

Recognizing negative thought patterns and cognitive distortions

The first step in cognitive restructuring is to become aware of the negative thought patterns and cognitive distortions that contribute to emotional distress and problematic behaviors. Negative thought patterns are habitual ways of thinking that are often automatic, distorted, and unhelpful. These thoughts can significantly influence our emotions and behaviors, perpetuating a cycle of distress and dysfunction.

Cognitive distortions are specific types of negative thought patterns that involve inaccurate or exaggerated interpretations of reality. Some common cognitive distortions include:

1. All-or-nothing thinking (also known as black-and-white thinking): This involves seeing things in extreme, absolute terms, with no middle ground. For example, someone with BPD might think, "If I'm not perfect, I'm a complete failure."

2. Overgeneralization: This involves drawing broad, negative conclusions based on a single event or limited evidence. For instance, if a person with BPD experiences a single rejection, they might conclude, "Nobody will ever love me."

3. Mental filter: This involves focusing exclusively on the negative aspects of a situation while ignoring or minimizing the positive aspects. Someone with BPD might dwell on a single critical comment while disregarding numerous compliments.

4. Emotional reasoning: This involves assuming that one's emotions reflect reality. For example, a person with BPD might think, "I feel guilty, so I must have done something wrong," even in the absence of evidence to support this conclusion.

5. Mind reading: This involves assuming that one knows what others are thinking, often projecting negative intentions onto their actions. Someone with BPD might assume, "My friend didn't return my text, so they must be angry with me," without considering alternative explanations.

Recognizing these negative thought patterns and cognitive distortions is crucial because they can significantly impact emotional well-being and behavior. When left unchallenged, these distorted thoughts can lead to intense emotions, impulsive reactions, and self-destructive behaviors.

For example, Sarah, who struggles with BPD, has a tendency towards all-or-nothing thinking. When her partner is late coming home from work, she immediately jumps to the conclusion, "He doesn't love me anymore. He's probably cheating on me." This thought leads to intense feelings of abandonment and rage, causing her to lash out at her partner when he arrives, leading to a heated argument and further relationship distress.

By learning to recognize negative thought patterns and cognitive distortions, individuals with BPD can begin to take the first steps towards challenging and modifying these thoughts, ultimately leading to improvements in emotional well-being and interpersonal relationships.

Learning techniques to challenge and reframe dysfunctional thoughts

Once individuals with BPD have learned to recognize their negative thought patterns and cognitive distortions, the next step is to challenge and reframe these dysfunctional thoughts. This process involves examining the evidence for and against the thought, considering alternative perspectives, and generating more balanced and realistic interpretations.

One effective technique for challenging dysfunctional thoughts is the "evidence for and against" method. This involves taking a specific thought and listing the evidence that supports it and the evidence that contradicts it. By objectively evaluating the evidence, individuals can begin to see the limitations and inaccuracies of their initial thought.

For example, Michael, who has BPD, often engages in overgeneralization. After a disagreement with a coworker, he thinks, "Everyone at work hates me. I'll never be able to succeed in my career." Using the "evidence for and against" method, Michael might list the following:

Evidence for:

• The coworker I disagreed with seemed upset with me.

• I sometimes feel like an outsider at work.

Evidence against:

• I have several coworkers who I get along with well.

• I recently received positive feedback from my supervisor on a project.

• I have been successful in my career thus far, despite occasional challenges.

By examining the evidence objectively, Michael can begin to see that his initial thought was an overgeneralization and not fully supported by the facts. This realization can help him generate a more balanced thought, such as, "While I may have occasional disagreements with coworkers, I have positive relationships with many people at work and have been successful in my career."

Another technique for challenging dysfunctional thoughts is cognitive reappraisal. This involves reframing a situation or thought in a more positive, realistic, or adaptive way. By looking at a situation from a different perspective, individuals can often find alternative interpretations that are less distressing and more constructive.

For instance, Emily, who struggles with BPD, frequently engages in emotional reasoning. When she feels anxious about a upcoming social event, she thinks, "I'm so nervous. I know I'm going to embarrass myself and everyone will hate me." Using cognitive reappraisal, Emily might reframe her thought as follows:

Original thought: "I'm so nervous. I know I'm going to embarrass myself and everyone will hate me."

Reframed thought: "It's normal to feel nervous before a social event. However, I have coping strategies I can use to manage my anxiety, and I have had positive social experiences in the past. Even if I do feel awkward at times, most people are understanding and not likely to judge me harshly."

By reframing her thought in a more realistic and compassionate way, Emily can reduce her anxiety and approach the social event with greater confidence and resilience.

It's important to note that challenging and reframing dysfunctional thoughts is a skill that requires practice and patience. It may feel unnatural or difficult at first, but with consistent effort, it can become a habitual way of responding to negative thought patterns. Over time, this process can lead to significant improvements in emotional well-being and behavioral functioning.

For example, Sarah, who previously struggled with all-or-nothing thinking, has been practicing cognitive restructuring techniques with her therapist. When her partner is late coming home from work, she still notices the initial thought, "He doesn't love me anymore. He's probably cheating on me." However, she now takes a moment to challenge this thought:

Original thought: "He doesn't love me anymore. He's probably cheating on me."

Challenged thought: "Just because he's late doesn't mean he doesn't love me. There could be many reasons for his delay, such as traffic or a last-minute work obligation. I know he loves me, and we have a strong relationship. I'll wait to hear his explanation before jumping to conclusions."

By challenging her initial thought and considering alternative explanations, Sarah is able to reduce her emotional distress and respond to the situation in a more adaptive manner. With continued practice, this way of thinking becomes more automatic, leading to lasting improvements in her emotional well-being and relationship functioning.

Practicing self-compassion and positive self-talk

In addition to challenging and reframing dysfunctional thoughts, practicing self-compassion and positive self-talk are essential components of cognitive restructuring for individuals with BPD. Self-compassion involves treating oneself with kindness, understanding, and acceptance, particularly in the face of difficult emotions or challenging circumstances. Positive self-talk involves engaging in supportive and encouraging inner dialogue, rather than harsh self-criticism or negative rumination.

Individuals with BPD often struggle with intense self-criticism and negative self-image. They may engage in habitual negative self-talk, such as "I'm worthless," "I'm a failure," or "I don't deserve love." This negative self-talk can perpetuate feelings of shame, guilt, and low self-esteem, exacerbating the emotional distress and interpersonal challenges associated with BPD.

Practicing self-compassion and positive self-talk can help counteract these negative patterns and promote emotional well-being. Self-compassion involves recognizing that all humans are imperfect and that struggles and setbacks are a normal part of life. By treating oneself with kindness and understanding, rather than harsh judgment, individuals can develop greater resilience and coping capacity.

For example, David, who has BPD, often engages in negative

self-talk when he makes a mistake at work. He thinks, "I'm so stupid. I can't do anything right. I deserve to be fired." By practicing self-compassion, David might respond to his mistake with a more supportive inner dialogue:

Original self-talk: "I'm so stupid. I can't do anything right. I deserve to be fired."

Self-compassionate response: "Everyone makes mistakes sometimes. It doesn't mean I'm stupid or incompetent. I'm human, and I'm learning. I'll take responsibility for my mistake, learn from it, and move forward. I deserve understanding and forgiveness, just like anyone else."

By treating himself with compassion and understanding, David can reduce his emotional distress and approach his mistake with a more constructive and resilient mindset.

Positive self-talk involves intentionally engaging in supportive and encouraging inner dialogue. This can involve acknowledging one's strengths, accomplishments, and positive qualities, as well as providing self-encouragement and motivation in the face of challenges.

For instance, Emily, who struggles with BPD, often criticizes herself harshly when she experiences interpersonal conflicts. She thinks, "I'm a terrible friend. No one will ever want to be close to me." By practicing positive self-talk, Emily can reframe her inner dialogue to be more supportive and encouraging:

Original self-talk: "I'm a terrible friend. No one will ever want to be close to me."

Positive self-talk: "I care deeply about my friends and try my best to be supportive. Conflicts are a normal part of any relationship, and they don't define my worth as a person. I have many positive qualities that make me a good friend, and I will continue to work on improving my communication and conflict-resolution skills."

By engaging in positive self-talk, Emily can bolster her self-esteem, reduce her emotional distress, and approach interpersonal challenges with greater confidence and resilience.

It's important to note that practicing self-compassion and positive self-talk may feel challenging or unnatural at first, particularly for individuals with BPD who have long-standing patterns of negative self-talk and self-criticism. However, with consistent practice and effort, these skills can become more habitual and automatic, leading to lasting improvements in emotional well-being and self-image.

For example, Sarah, who previously struggled with intense self-criticism and negative self-talk, has been working with her therapist to cultivate self-compassion and positive self-talk. Initially, she found it difficult to generate supportive and encouraging inner dialogue, often falling back into patterns of self-judgment and criticism. However, with practice and persistence, she began to notice a shift in her inner voice:

Original self-talk: "I'm a failure. I'll never be good enough."

Self-compassionate response: "I'm doing the best I can, and that's all anyone can ask for. I'm learning and growing every day, and I deserve to be kind and patient with myself, just as I would be with a good friend."

As Sarah continues to practice self-compassion and positive self-talk, she finds that these supportive and encouraging messages become more automatic and easily accessible, even in the face of challenges or setbacks. This shift in her inner dialogue contributes to significant improvements in her self-esteem, emotional resilience, and overall well-being.

In conclusion, identifying and challenging dysfunctional thoughts through techniques such as cognitive restructuring, self-compassion, and positive self-talk are crucial components of Cognitive Behavioral Therapy (CBT) for individuals with Borderline Personality Disorder (BPD). By learning to recognize negative thought patterns and cognitive distortions, individuals can take the first step towards modifying these unhelpful ways of thinking.

Through techniques such as examining the evidence for and against a thought, considering alternative perspectives, and reframing situations in a more balanced and realistic way, individuals with BPD can begin to challenge and modify their dysfunctional thoughts. This process can lead to significant improvements in emotional well-being, interpersonal relationships, and overall functioning.

Furthermore, by cultivating self-compassion and engaging in positive self-talk, individuals with BPD can counteract patterns of intense self-criticism and negative self-image. Treating oneself with kindness, understanding, and encouragement can promote greater emotional resilience, self-esteem, and coping capacity.

While learning and implementing these techniques may feel challenging at first, with consistent practice and effort, they can become habitual and automatic ways of responding to negative thought patterns. Over time, this cognitive restructuring can contribute to lasting improvements in emotional well-being, behavioral functioning, and overall quality of life for individuals with BPD.

It is important to remember that cognitive restructuring is a gradual process that requires patience, self-compassion, and a willingness to confront and modify long-standing patterns of thinking. With the guidance and support of a trained CBT therapist, individuals with BPD can develop the skills and strategies needed to effectively identify, challenge, and reframe their dysfunctional thoughts, ultimately leading to a more balanced, resilient, and fulfilling life.

4

Regulating Intense Emotions: Strategies for Emotional Regulation and Distress Tolerance

Emotional dysregulation is a core feature of Borderline Personality Disorder (BPD), characterized by intense, rapidly shifting emotions that can be difficult to manage. Individuals with BPD often experience emotions more intensely and for longer durations than those without the disorder, leading to significant distress and impairment in daily functioning. In this chapter, we will explore the role of emotions in BPD, learn strategies for identifying and labeling emotions, and develop skills for managing intense emotions and tolerating distress.

Understanding the role of emotions in BPD

Emotions serve important functions in our lives, providing information about our experiences, guiding our decision-making, and motivating us to take action. However, for individuals with BPD, emotions can feel overwhelming, unpredictable, and uncontrollable, leading to a range of negative consequences.

One key aspect of emotional dysregulation in BPD is emotional sensitivity. Individuals with BPD may be highly attuned to emotional cues in their environment, quickly detecting and reacting to perceived threats or slights. This heightened sensitivity can lead to frequent and intense emotional reactions, even in response to relatively minor stressors.

For example, Sarah, who has BPD, may be having a conversation with a friend who seems slightly distracted. While most people might not notice or be bothered by this, Sarah immediately perceives it as a sign that her friend is upset with her or losing interest in their friendship. This perception triggers an intense emotional response, such as feelings of abandonment, anger, or despair, which can quickly escalate and lead to impulsive behaviors or interpersonal conflicts.

Another aspect of emotional dysregulation in BPD is emotional reactivity. Individuals with BPD may experience rapid and extreme shifts in their emotions, moving from one intense emotion to another in a short period of time. This emotional lability can be challenging to navigate, both for the individual experiencing it and for those around them.

For instance, Michael, who struggles with BPD, may wake up feeling content and excited about his day. However, a minor setback at work, such as a perceived criticism from his boss, can quickly trigger a shift to intense feelings of worthlessness and despair. These emotions may then give way to anger and frustration, leading Michael to lash out at his coworkers or engage in self-destructive behaviors to cope with his distress.

The intensity and duration of emotions in BPD can also be problematic. Individuals with BPD may experience emotions that feel unbearable and all-consuming, lasting for extended periods without relief. This persistent emotional distress can lead to a sense of desperation and a desire to escape or numb the painful feelings by any means necessary.

Emily, who has BPD, may experience a breakup with a romantic partner as utterly devastating. The intensity of her grief and despair may feel unbearable, lasting for weeks or even months without respite. During this time, she may struggle to engage in daily activities, such as work or self-care, and may turn to maladaptive coping strategies, such as substance abuse or self-harm, in an attempt to escape her emotional pain.

The emotional dysregulation associated with BPD can have significant negative impacts on various domains of life. Intense and unstable emotions can lead to impulsive behaviors, such as reckless spending, substance abuse, or risky sexual practices, which can have harmful consequences for physical and mental health. Emotional dysregulation can also strain interpersonal relationships, leading to frequent conflicts, breakups, and a sense of isolation and loneliness.

Moreover, the persistent emotional distress experienced by individuals with BPD can contribute to the development of co-occurring mental health conditions, such as depression, anxiety disorders, and substance use disorders. These conditions can further exacerbate the emotional dysregulation and overall impairment associated with BPD.

Given the significant impact of emotional dysregulation on the lives of individuals with BPD, developing effective strategies for emotional regulation and distress tolerance is crucial. By learning to identify, understand, and manage intense emotions, individuals with BPD can reduce their distress, improve their functioning, and build more stable and satisfying lives.

Learning strategies for identifying and labeling emotions

The first step in effectively managing emotions is developing the ability to accurately identify and label them. For individuals with BPD, who may experience intense and rapidly shifting emotions, this can be a challenging but essential skill.

One common difficulty for people with BPD is distinguishing between different emotions. They may experience a general sense of distress or overwhelming emotion without being able to pinpoint the specific feelings they are experiencing. This lack of emotional clarity can make it harder to address and regulate emotions effectively.

To improve emotional awareness, individuals with BPD can practice mindfulness techniques, which involve paying attention to the present moment with openness, curiosity, and non-judgment. By tuning into their physical sensations, thoughts, and feelings, they can begin to develop a clearer sense of their emotional experiences.

For example, Sarah, who struggles with identifying her

emotions, may take a few minutes each day to practice a mindfulness exercise. She might sit quietly and focus on her breath, noticing any physical sensations, such as tightness in her chest or a knot in her stomach. She may also observe any thoughts or feelings that arise, without trying to change or suppress them. Over time, this practice can help Sarah become more attuned to her emotional experiences and better able to differentiate between different feelings.

Another helpful strategy for identifying emotions is to use an "emotion wheel" or a list of emotion words. These tools provide a visual representation or a comprehensive list of various emotions, which can help individuals pinpoint and name their specific feelings.

Michael, who often struggles to put his emotions into words, may find an emotion wheel particularly useful. When he experiences a strong emotion, he can refer to the wheel to help him identify the specific feeling he is experiencing. For instance, if he is feeling a general sense of discomfort, he may look at the wheel and realize that he is actually feeling a combination of frustration, disappointment, and anxiety. By naming these specific emotions, Michael can gain a clearer understanding of his experience and begin to explore the thoughts and situations that may be contributing to these feelings.

Labeling emotions accurately is important because it allows individuals to communicate their experiences more effectively to others and to themselves. By putting feelings into words, individuals with BPD can gain a sense of validation and self-understanding, as well as help others understand and empathize with their experiences.

Emily, who has BPD, may have difficulty expressing her emotions to her loved ones, often feeling misunderstood or dismissed. By learning to label her emotions more precisely, she can communicate her needs and experiences more clearly. For example, instead of simply saying, "I feel bad," Emily might say, "I'm feeling overwhelmed and anxious right now, and I could really use some support and understanding." This clear communication can help her loved ones respond more effectively and compassionately to her needs.

In addition to promoting effective communication, labeling emotions can also help individuals with BPD gain a sense of control over their experiences. By naming an emotion, they can begin to separate themselves from it, recognizing that they are experiencing an emotion rather than being defined by it.

For instance, when Sarah is able to identify that she is feeling intense anger, she can remind herself, "I am experiencing anger right now, but anger is not who I am. I can choose how to respond to this feeling." This perspective can help Sarah feel more empowered and less controlled by her emotions, enabling her to make healthier choices in response to her feelings.

Learning to identify and label emotions is a foundational skill for emotional regulation and distress tolerance. By developing this skill through practices such as mindfulness, using emotion wheels or word lists, and communicating feelings to others, individuals with BPD can gain a clearer understanding of their emotional experiences, feel more in control of their responses, and build more effective coping strategies.

Developing skills for managing intense emotions and tolerating distress

Once individuals with BPD have learned to identify and label their emotions, the next step is to develop skills for managing intense emotions and tolerating distress. These skills are essential for reducing the negative impact of emotional dysregulation on daily life and promoting overall well-being.

One key skill for managing intense emotions is emotion regulation. Emotion regulation involves strategies for modifying the intensity or duration of emotional experiences, as well as the behavioral responses to those emotions. By learning to regulate their emotions effectively, individuals with BPD can reduce their distress and improve their ability to function in daily life.

One emotion regulation strategy is deep breathing. Deep breathing involves taking slow, deliberate breaths from the diaphragm, which can help calm the body's physiological response to intense emotions. By focusing on the breath and slowing down the breathing rate, individuals can reduce feelings of anxiety, anger, or overwhelm.

For example, when Michael notices that he is starting to feel intense anger during a conversation with his boss, he may take a moment to practice deep breathing. He might excuse himself from the conversation briefly, find a quiet place, and take several slow, deep breaths. As he focuses on his breath, he may notice his heart rate slowing down and his muscles relaxing. This simple strategy can help Michael regain a sense of calm and control, allowing him to respond to the situation more effectively.

Another emotion regulation strategy is progressive muscle relaxation. This technique involves systematically tensing and relaxing different muscle groups in the body, which can help reduce physical tension and promote a sense of relaxation. By learning to identify and release tension in the body, individuals with BPD can reduce the physical sensations associated with intense emotions and promote a greater sense of emotional control.

Sarah, who struggles with intense anxiety, may practice progressive muscle relaxation regularly as part of her self-care routine. She might set aside 10-15 minutes each day to work through the different muscle groups, tensing each one for several seconds before releasing the tension and focusing on the sensation of relaxation. Over time, this practice can help Sarah become more aware of her body's response to stress and develop a greater sense of control over her physical and emotional experiences.

In addition to emotion regulation strategies, individuals with BPD can also benefit from learning distress tolerance skills. Distress tolerance involves the ability to withstand and cope with intense emotional or physical discomfort without resorting to maladaptive behaviors or impulsive actions. By developing distress tolerance, individuals with BPD can learn to ride out intense emotions without making their situations worse.

One distress tolerance skill is distraction. Distraction involves intentionally shifting attention away from distressing thoughts or emotions and focusing on something else. This can include engaging in enjoyable activities, such as reading a book, listening to music, or going for a walk, as well as focusing on sensory experiences, such as the taste of a favorite food or the sensation of a warm bath.

Emily, who often experiences intense feelings of sadness and emptiness, may use distraction as a way to cope with her distress without turning to self-destructive behaviors. When she notices these difficult emotions arising, she might choose to call a friend, work on a puzzle, or engage in a creative hobby like painting. By intentionally shifting her focus to something else, Emily can give herself a break from her distressing emotions and reduce the urge to engage in harmful behaviors.

Another distress tolerance skill is self-soothing. Self-soothing involves engaging in activities that promote a sense of comfort, safety, and well-being. This can include physical self-care activities, such as taking a warm bath or applying lotion, as well as mental self-care activities, such as repeating a calming mantra or visualizing a peaceful scene.

Michael, who struggles with intense feelings of worthlessness and self-loathing, may use self-soothing techniques to cope with these painful emotions. He might keep a list of comforting activities, such as listening to his favorite music, wrapping himself in a soft blanket, or looking at pictures of loved ones, and turn to these activities when he is feeling distressed. By engaging in self-soothing, Michael can counteract his negative emotions with a sense of self-compassion and care.

Developing effective skills for managing intense emotions and tolerating distress takes time and practice. It is important for individuals with BPD to work with a mental health professional, such as a therapist trained in Dialectical Behavior Therapy (DBT), to learn and practice these skills in a supportive environment. With consistent practice and support, individuals with BPD can build a toolkit of strategies for coping with intense emotions and distress, allowing them to lead more stable and fulfilling lives.

It is also important to recognize that emotional regulation and distress tolerance skills are not about eliminating difficult emotions altogether. Rather, these skills are about learning to respond to emotions in a more effective and healthy way, reducing the negative impact of intense emotions on daily life and relationships. By developing a greater sense of control over their emotional experiences, individuals with BPD can build resilience and improve their overall quality of life.

Furthermore, it is crucial to approach the development of these skills with self-compassion and patience. Learning to manage intense emotions and tolerate distress is a gradual process, and setbacks are a normal part of the journey. By treating themselves with kindness and understanding, individuals with BPD can maintain motivation and commitment to the process of building emotional regulation and distress tolerance skills.

In addition to individual skill-building, it is also important to consider the role of social support in emotional regulation and distress tolerance. Having a network of supportive friends, family members, or professionals can provide a sense of connection and validation that can be invaluable in coping with intense emotions. By reaching out for help and support when needed, individuals with BPD can reduce their sense of isolation and build a greater sense of emotional resilience.

In conclusion, developing skills for managing intense emotions and tolerating distress is a crucial aspect of treatment for Borderline Personality Disorder. By learning strategies such as emotion regulation techniques, distress tolerance skills, and self-compassion, individuals with BPD can gain a greater sense of control over their emotional experiences and reduce the negative impact of emotional dysregulation on their lives.

Through consistent practice and support, individuals with BPD can build a toolkit of effective coping strategies, allowing them to navigate the challenges of intense emotions with greater resilience and stability. By approaching this process with patience, self-compassion, and a willingness to seek support when needed, individuals with BPD can work towards a more fulfilling and satisfying life, characterized by improved emotional well-being and stronger, more stable relationships.

5

Improving Interpersonal Relationships: Communication Skills and Boundary Setting

Interpersonal relationships are an essential part of our lives, providing us with emotional support, a sense of belonging, and opportunities for personal growth. However, for individuals with Borderline Personality Disorder (BPD), navigating relationships can be particularly challenging. BPD is characterized by intense and unstable relationships, fear of abandonment, and difficulty with emotional regulation, all of which can lead to patterns of conflict, misunderstandings, and broken connections. In this chapter, we will explore the impact of BPD on relationships, learn effective communication techniques, and discuss the importance of setting and maintaining healthy boundaries.

Exploring the impact of BPD on relationships

BPD can have a significant impact on interpersonal relationships, affecting the way individuals interact with family members, friends, romantic partners, and colleagues. The core features of BPD, such as emotional instability, impulsivity, and an unstable sense of self, can create a turbulent and unpredictable relational landscape, leading to frequent misunderstandings, conflicts, and breakups.

One of the primary ways BPD impacts relationships is through the fear of abandonment. Individuals with BPD may be hyper-vigilant to signs of potential rejection or abandonment, often interpreting neutral or ambiguous situations as threatening. This fear can lead to clingy or desperate behaviors, such as constantly seeking reassurance, making frantic efforts to prevent the person from leaving, or even resorting to manipulation or threats to keep the relationship intact.

For example, Sarah, who has BPD, may become extremely anxious when her boyfriend doesn't respond to her text messages within a few minutes. She might start catastrophizing, thinking, "He's probably tired of me and wants to break up." Driven by her fear of abandonment, Sarah might send a barrage of increasingly frantic messages, call him repeatedly, or even show up at his workplace uninvited, all in an attempt to get a response and reassurance that he still cares about her.

This fear of abandonment can also lead to a pattern of pushing people away. Individuals with BPD may engage in behavior that sabotages relationships, such as picking fights, becoming overly critical, or abruptly ending the relationship before the other person has a chance to leave them. This "push-pull" dynamic can be confusing and exhausting for the people in their lives, who may feel like they are constantly walking on eggshells, never knowing what to expect.

Another way BPD can impact relationships is through the phenomenon of "splitting." Splitting refers to the tendency to see people or situations in black-and-white terms, as either all good or all bad. For individuals with BPD, there is often no middle ground – a person is either idealized as perfect and loving or devalued as cruel and rejecting.

For instance, Michael, who struggles with BPD, may put his new girlfriend on a pedestal, believing she is the most amazing person he has ever met. He might spend all his time with her, shower her with affection and gifts, and share his deepest secrets and vulnerabilities. However, the moment she does something that disappoints him, such as canceling a date due to illness, Michael may abruptly switch to seeing her as uncaring and selfish. He might lash out at her, accuse her of not loving him, or even end the relationship in a fit of anger.

This pattern of idealization and devaluation can be highly destabilizing for relationships, as it creates an atmosphere of uncertainty and emotional whiplash. The people in the lives of individuals with BPD may feel like they can never live up to the idealized image and are constantly at risk of being devalued and rejected.

The emotional intensity and reactivity associated with BPD can also contribute to relationship difficulties. Individuals with BPD may experience emotions more intensely and have a harder time regulating their emotional responses. This can lead to frequent emotional outbursts, intense arguments, and impulsive behaviors that can strain relationships.

Emily, who has BPD, may be highly sensitive to any perceived criticism or slight from her friends. If a friend makes a casual joke at her expense, Emily might experience intense hurt and anger, leading her to lash out or give her friend the silent treatment for days. This emotional reactivity can make it challenging for Emily to maintain stable, long-term friendships, as her friends may grow weary of constantly having to monitor their words and actions to avoid triggering an emotional response.

The impact of BPD on relationships can be further compounded by co-occurring mental health conditions, such as depression, anxiety, or substance use disorders. These conditions can exacerbate the symptoms of BPD and contribute to additional relational challenges, such as social withdrawal, increased conflict, or a lack of trust.

It is important to recognize that the relational difficulties associated with BPD are not intentional or manipulative. Rather, they are the result of deep-seated fears, intense emotions, and maladaptive coping strategies that have often developed in response to early experiences of trauma, neglect, or invalidation. By understanding the impact of BPD on relationships, individuals with BPD and their loved ones can develop greater empathy, patience, and commitment to working together to build healthier, more stable connections.

Learning effective communication techniques

Effective communication is essential for building and maintaining healthy relationships. For individuals with BPD, who may struggle with emotional reactivity and interpersonal challenges, learning effective communication techniques can be particularly important. By developing skills for expressing needs, listening actively, and managing conflict, individuals with BPD can improve the quality of their relationships and reduce the frequency and intensity of relational difficulties.

One key aspect of effective communication is learning to express needs and feelings clearly and directly. Individuals with BPD may have difficulty identifying and articulating their emotions, leading them to communicate through indirect or passive-aggressive means. They may hint at their needs, expecting others to read their minds, or they may bottle up their feelings until they explode in a burst of intense emotion.

To improve communication, individuals with BPD can practice using "I" statements to express their feelings and needs. "I" statements focus on expressing one's own experiences, rather than making accusations or assumptions about the other person. For example, instead of saying, "You never listen to me," which can come across as an attack, an individual might say, "I feel unheard when I'm trying to share my thoughts with you. Can we find a time to talk when you're able to give me your full attention?" By expressing needs and feelings directly and non-judgmentally, individuals with BPD can reduce misunderstandings and increase the likelihood of having their needs met.

Active listening is another crucial communication skill. Active listening involves giving one's full attention to the speaker, seeking to understand their perspective, and reflecting back what has been heard. For individuals with BPD, who may be prone to emotional reactivity and impulsive responses, practicing active listening can help them stay grounded in the present moment and respond more effectively to others.

When practicing active listening, it is important to minimize distractions, maintain eye contact, and show interest through nonverbal cues such as nodding or leaning in. Individuals can also use reflective statements to clarify their understanding, such as, "What I'm hearing is that you feel overwhelmed by your workload and need some support. Is that accurate?" By demonstrating that they are fully present and engaged in the conversation, individuals with BPD can foster a sense of connection and understanding in their relationships.

Managing conflict is another important aspect of effective communication. Conflicts are a normal part of any relationship, but for individuals with BPD, who may have a lower tolerance for distress and a tendency towards emotional reactivity, conflicts can quickly escalate and become destructive. Learning to approach conflicts with a problem-solving mindset, rather than a combative one, can help individuals with BPD navigate disagreements more successfully.

One technique for managing conflict is to focus on using "we" language, which emphasizes collaboration and shared responsibility. For example, instead of saying, "You always make me feel bad about myself," an individual might say, "I feel like we've been struggling to communicate lately, and it's causing a lot of hurt feelings. Can we work together to find a way to express ourselves more kindly?" By framing conflicts as a shared challenge to be tackled together, rather than a battle to be won, individuals with BPD can reduce defensiveness and increase cooperation.

It can also be helpful to practice taking breaks during conflicts, especially when emotions are running high. Taking a few minutes to step away from the conversation, engage in a calming activity, and collect one's thoughts can help individuals with BPD regain emotional equilibrium and respond more effectively. It is important to communicate the need for a break clearly and respectfully, with a commitment to returning to the conversation when ready. For example, an individual might say, "I'm feeling very overwhelmed right now, and I need a few minutes to calm down. Can we take a 15-minute break and then come back to discuss this?"

In addition to these specific techniques, individuals with BPD can also benefit from practicing general communication skills, such as maintaining an open and curious attitude, avoiding assumptions or mind-reading, and being willing to compromise and find mutually satisfying solutions. By approaching communication as a learnable skill set, rather than an innate ability, individuals with BPD can develop greater confidence and competence in their interpersonal interactions.

Learning effective communication techniques takes time, practice, and patience. It is important for individuals with BPD to be gentle with themselves as they work to develop these skills, recognizing that setbacks and mistakes are a normal part of the learning process. Seeking support from a therapist, particularly one trained in Dialectical Behavior Therapy (DBT), can provide a safe and supportive environment for practicing communication skills and receiving feedback and guidance.

In addition to individual skill-building, it can also be helpful for individuals with BPD to involve their loved ones in the process of learning effective communication. By sharing their goals and strategies with family members, friends, or romantic partners, individuals with BPD can create a shared understanding and commitment to improving communication patterns. Loved ones can offer support, encouragement, and gentle feedback as individuals with BPD practice their new skills in real-world interactions.

Ultimately, learning effective communication techniques is about more than just exchanging information or managing conflicts. It is about building deeper, more authentic connections with others, based on mutual understanding, respect, and care. By investing in the development of these skills, individuals with BPD can create more fulfilling and sustainable relationships, enhancing their overall quality of life and sense of well-being.

Setting and maintaining healthy boundaries in relationships

In addition to learning effective communication techniques, setting and maintaining healthy boundaries is another critical aspect of improving interpersonal relationships for individuals with BPD. Boundaries refer to the physical, emotional, and mental limits we set to protect our well-being and maintain a sense of autonomy in our relationships. For individuals with BPD, who may struggle with an unstable sense of self and a fear of abandonment, setting and maintaining boundaries can be particularly challenging, but also especially important.

One common boundary difficulty for individuals with BPD is a tendency towards over-sharing or over-involvement in others' lives. In an effort to create closeness and prevent abandonment, individuals with BPD may share too much personal information too quickly, or become excessively involved in the problems or emotions of others. This can lead to a sense of enmeshment or codependency, where the individual with BPD loses sight of their own needs and identity in the process of trying to maintain the relationship.

For example, Emily, who has BPD, may have a tendency to dive headfirst into new friendships, sharing her deepest secrets and insecurities within the first few interactions. She may also take on her friends' problems as her own, staying up late to talk them through their relationship struggles or offering to help them with tasks that drain her own time and energy. While Emily's intentions may be good, this lack of boundaries can leave her feeling exhausted, overwhelmed, and resentful, as well as create an unhealthy dynamic where her friends come to rely on her too heavily.

To set healthier boundaries around over-sharing and over-involvement, individuals with BPD can practice taking things more slowly in new relationships, gradually building trust and intimacy over time. They can also learn to check in with themselves before offering help or support, asking, "Is this something I have the time, energy, and resources to take on right now? Will saying yes to this request come at the cost of my own well-being?" By becoming more mindful of their own limits and needs, individuals with BPD can develop a stronger sense of self and create more balanced, mutually supportive relationships.

Another boundary challenge for individuals with BPD is difficulty tolerating separateness or alone time in relationships. The fear of abandonment can be so strong that individuals with BPD may feel a constant need to be in contact with their loved ones, becoming anxious or upset when they are not immediately available. They may engage in frantic efforts to maintain connection, such as sending a barrage of texts or showing up uninvited, which can feel overwhelming or intrusive to others.

Michael, who struggles with BPD, may have a hard time when his girlfriend goes out with her friends for the evening. Despite her reassurances that she will be back later, Michael may find himself consumed with anxiety and a sense of impending abandonment. He may send her multiple messages throughout the night, asking when she will be home or accusing her of not caring about him. When she finally returns, he may be sullen and withdrawn, or pick a fight as a way of expressing his hurt and fear.

To set healthier boundaries around separateness, individuals with BPD can work on developing a stronger sense of self and self-soothing strategies for managing anxiety and distress. This may involve engaging in solo activities that bring a sense of joy, accomplishment, or relaxation, such as pursuing a hobby, practicing mindfulness, or journaling. It can also be helpful to practice gradually increasing the amount of time spent apart from loved ones, building up tolerance and trust in the relationship's ability to withstand distance.

Finally, individuals with BPD may struggle with setting boundaries around their own emotional needs and limits. They may have a hard time saying no to requests, setting limits on their availability, or communicating when they are feeling overwhelmed or depleted. This can lead to a pattern of self-sacrifice and burnout, as well as resentment towards others for not respecting their unspoken needs.

Sarah, who has BPD, may find herself consistently putting her own needs last in her relationships. She may agree to help a friend move, even when she is already exhausted from work, or stay up late comforting a family member, even though she has an important meeting in the morning. Over time, this lack of boundaries can leave Sarah feeling drained, unappreciated, and even angry at her loved ones for not reciprocating her level of devotion.

To set healthier boundaries around emotional needs and limits, individuals with BPD can practice tuning into their own feelings and body sensations, learning to recognize the signs of emotional depletion or overwhelm. They can also work on communicating their needs and limits clearly and directly, using "I" statements and assertive language. For example, Sarah might say, "I care about you and want to be there for you, but I'm feeling really overwhelmed right now and need some time to recharge. Can we find another time to talk when I'm feeling more rested?" By learning to prioritize their own self-care and communicate their needs, individuals with BPD can develop more sustainable and satisfying relationships.

It is important to recognize that setting and maintaining healthy boundaries is a process, not a one-time event. It requires ongoing self-reflection, communication, and adjustment, as individuals with BPD navigate the complexities of their relationships and their own changing needs. It is also important to be prepared for some discomfort or pushback from others as boundaries are established, as loved ones may need time to adjust to new patterns of interaction.

Seeking support from a therapist can be invaluable in the process of learning to set and maintain healthy boundaries. A therapist can provide guidance, role-playing opportunities, and a safe space to process any challenges or setbacks that arise. They can also help individuals with BPD develop a clearer sense of their own values, needs, and limits, which can serve as a foundation for creating healthier relationships.

Ultimately, setting and maintaining healthy boundaries is about honoring oneself and one's relationships. It is about creating a balance between giving and receiving, between connection and autonomy, and between self-care and care for others. By learning to set and maintain healthy boundaries, individuals with BPD can develop a stronger sense of self, improve the quality of their relationships, and enhance their overall well-being and life satisfaction.

In conclusion, improving interpersonal relationships is a crucial aspect of treatment and recovery for individuals with Borderline Personality Disorder. BPD can have a significant impact on relationships, leading to patterns of instability, conflict, and pain. However, by learning effective communication techniques and setting and maintaining healthy boundaries, individuals with BPD can develop the skills and strategies needed to build more fulfilling and sustainable connections.

Effective communication involves learning to express needs and feelings clearly and directly, practicing active listening, and managing conflict with a collaborative, problem-solving approach. It requires a willingness to be vulnerable, to take responsibility for one's own thoughts and feelings, and to approach others with empathy and respect.

Setting and maintaining healthy boundaries involves learning to recognize and honor one's own needs, limits, and values, while also respecting the autonomy and needs of others. It requires developing a strong sense of self, communicating assertively, and being willing to tolerate some discomfort or pushback as new patterns of interaction are established.

Both effective communication and healthy boundaries are learnable skills that can be developed and strengthened over time, with practice, patience, and support. By seeking guidance from a therapist, involving loved ones in the process of change, and approaching the work with self-compassion and a growth mindset, individuals with BPD can transform their relationships and their lives.

Ultimately improving interpersonal relationships is about more than just reducing conflict or increasing stability. It is about creating a sense of genuine connection, mutual understanding, and shared growth. When individuals with BPD learn to communicate effectively and set healthy boundaries, they open up the possibility for deeper, more authentic relationships, based on trust, respect, and care.

The benefits of this work extend far beyond the realm of interpersonal relationships. As individuals with BPD develop a stronger sense of self and a greater capacity for healthy connection, they may also experience improvements in their mental health, self-esteem, and overall quality of life. They may feel more empowered to pursue their goals, to assert their needs, and to engage with the world in a more fulfilling and meaningful way.

Moreover, the ripple effects of this work can extend outward, positively impacting the lives of loved ones and communities. As individuals with BPD model healthy communication and boundaries, they create opportunities for others to learn and grow alongside them. They may inspire greater empathy, understanding, and resilience in their families, friendships, and romantic partnerships, contributing to a wider culture of emotional well-being and relational health.

It is important to acknowledge that the journey of improving interpersonal relationships is not always a straight or easy path. There may be setbacks, challenges, and moments of discouragement along the way. However, with commitment, support, and a willingness to learn from both successes and struggles, individuals with BPD can make profound and lasting changes in their relational lives.

In many ways, the work of improving interpersonal relationships is the work of a lifetime. It requires ongoing self-reflection, skill-building, and adaptation, as individuals navigate the ever-changing landscape of their lives and connections. However, it is work that is deeply worthwhile, as it holds the potential for greater joy, meaning, and fulfilment in all areas of life.

For individuals with BPD who are embarking on this journey, it can be helpful to hold onto a vision of the kind of relationships they want to create – relationships characterized by mutual care, respect, and understanding. By keeping this vision in mind, and by taking small steps each day to communicate more effectively and set healthier boundaries, individuals with BPD can gradually transform their relational world from a source of pain and instability to a source of comfort, growth, and healing.

In the end, improving interpersonal relationships is not just about changing behaviours or developing new skills. It is about claiming one's inherent worth, dignity, and right to be treated with love and respect. It is about learning to honour oneself and others, and to create a life filled with connection, meaning, and joy. For individuals with BPD, this work may be challenging, but it is also profoundly empowering and transformative, holding the key to a brighter, more fulfilling future.

6

Developing a Stronger Sense of Self: Identity, Self-Image, and Self-Esteem

A strong and stable sense of self is a crucial foundation for emotional well-being and healthy relationships. It provides us with a clear understanding of who we are, what we value, and how we want to engage with the world around us. However, for individuals with Borderline Personality Disorder (BPD), developing and maintaining a coherent sense of self can be a significant challenge. BPD is often characterized by identity disturbances, negative self-image, and low self-esteem, which can contribute to emotional instability, impulsive behaviors, and interpersonal difficulties. In this chapter, we will explore the nature of identity disturbances in BPD, discuss strategies for developing a more stable and positive sense of self, and examine the importance of building self-esteem and self-confidence.

Understanding identity disturbances in BPD

Identity disturbances are a core feature of BPD, reflecting a profound difficulty in establishing and maintaining a clear, consistent, and positive sense of self. Individuals with BPD often report feeling like they don't know who they are, what they believe in, or what they want out of life. They may describe their sense of self as shifting, fragmented, or empty, leading to a chronic feeling of instability and inner turmoil.

One manifestation of identity disturbances in BPD is a tendency towards role absorption. Individuals with BPD may quickly and intensely adopt the identities, values, or interests of those around them, especially in new relationships or social situations. They may become so absorbed in the role of "perfect partner," "devoted friend," or "successful professional" that they lose sight of their own authentic thoughts, feelings, and needs.

For example, Sarah, who struggles with BPD, has always had a hard time figuring out who she is and what she stands for. When she starts a new job, she quickly becomes consumed by the role of "ideal employee," working long hours, taking on extra projects, and mimicking the communication style of her colleagues. While this earns her praise and recognition at work, it leaves her feeling drained and disconnected from herself. Outside of work, Sarah finds herself adopting the hobbies and opinions of her new group of friends, even when they don't align with her own interests or values. As a result, she feels like a chameleon, always changing to fit in, but never quite sure of who she really is.

Another aspect of identity disturbances in BPD is a lack of self-continuity, or a sense that one's identity is constantly shifting or unstable over time. Individuals with BPD may have difficulty integrating past experiences, present circumstances, and future aspirations into a coherent narrative of self. They may feel like they are radically different people from one day to the next, or even from one moment to the next, leading to a sense of inner chaos and unpredictability.

Michael, who has BPD, often feels like his sense of self is a moving target. On some days, he feels confident, outgoing, and optimistic, pursuing his goals with enthusiasm and drive. On other days, he feels worthless, anxious, and hopeless, questioning every decision he's ever made and doubting his ability to create a meaningful life. These rapid shifts in identity leave Michael feeling exhausted and confused, never quite sure which version of himself is the "real" one. In his relationships, he often feels like he's playing a role, rather than authentically connecting with others, further compounding his sense of self-doubt and instability.

Identity disturbances in BPD can be further complicated by a tendency towards black-and-white thinking, or splitting. Individuals with BPD may view themselves in extreme, all-or-nothing terms, seeing themselves as either completely good or completely bad, with no shades of gray in between. This polarized self-image can lead to rapid shifts in self-esteem, as well as impulsive behaviors aimed at proving or disproving these extreme self-perceptions.

Emily, who struggles with BPD, has a hard time maintaining a balanced and compassionate view of herself. When she receives positive feedback or achieves a goal, she feels like she's on top of the world, a shining example of success and worth. However, the moment she encounters a setback or criticism, she plummets into self-loathing, convinced that she's a total failure and a burden to others. These extreme swings in self-image leave Emily feeling trapped in a cycle of euphoria and despair, never quite able to find a stable middle ground.

The root causes of identity disturbances in BPD are complex and multifaceted, often stemming from a combination of genetic, environmental, and developmental factors. Early experiences of trauma, neglect, or invalidation can disrupt the normal process of identity formation, leaving individuals with BPD without a secure base from which to explore and define themselves. Inconsistent or unpredictable caregiving, as well as a lack of positive role models or reflective mirroring, can further contribute to a fragmented or underdeveloped sense of self.

Moreover, the intense and rapidly shifting emotions associated with BPD can make it difficult for individuals to maintain a stable self-concept. When emotions feel overwhelming or out of control, it can be challenging to hold onto a clear and consistent sense of who one is, what one values, or how one wants to live. The constant emotional turmoil can create a sense of inner chaos and confusion, further exacerbating identity disturbances.

It's important to recognize that identity disturbances in BPD are not a choice or a character flaw, but rather a reflection of complex developmental and emotional challenges. By understanding the nature and origins of these disturbances, individuals with BPD can begin to develop self-compassion and a sense of hope for positive change. With the right support, strategies, and resources, it is possible to build a stronger, more stable, and more positive sense of self, even in the face of significant identity challenges.

Developing a more stable and positive sense of self

Developing a more stable and positive sense of self is a key goal of treatment for individuals with BPD. While identity disturbances can feel overwhelming and entrenched, there are many strategies and techniques that can help individuals build a clearer, more consistent, and more compassionate self-concept. These strategies involve a combination of self-reflection, skill-building, and experiential learning, all aimed at fostering a greater sense of self-awareness, self-acceptance, and self-direction.

One important strategy for developing a more stable sense of self is to engage in regular self-reflection and self-exploration. This involves taking time to examine one's thoughts, feelings, values, and experiences, with an attitude of curiosity and non-judgment. By becoming more aware of one's inner world, individuals with BPD can begin to identify patterns, themes, and core aspects of self that may have been previously overlooked or underdeveloped.

Journaling is one powerful tool for self-reflection and self-exploration. By setting aside time each day to write about one's experiences, emotions, and insights, individuals can gain a greater sense of clarity and perspective on their lives. Prompt questions such as "What are three things I value most in life?" or "What are some of my unique strengths and qualities?" can help guide the self-reflection process and uncover important aspects of identity.

For Sarah, who struggles with role absorption and a lack of self-continuity, journaling has become a daily practice for self-discovery. Each morning, she sets aside 20 minutes to write about her thoughts, feelings, and experiences, without censoring or judging herself. Over time, she begins to notice patterns in her writing, such as a deep love of nature, a passion for social justice, and a fear of abandonment. These insights help Sarah develop a clearer sense of who she is and what matters most to her, separate from the roles and expectations of others. As she continues to explore her inner world through journaling, Sarah feels a growing sense of self-awareness and self-acceptance, which helps her navigate life with greater stability and purpose.

Another strategy for developing a more stable sense of self is to engage in values clarification and goal-setting. This involves identifying one's core values, or the guiding principles that give life meaning and direction, and setting specific, achievable goals that align with these values. By clarifying what matters most and taking concrete steps towards a valued life, individuals with BPD can develop a stronger sense of self-direction and purpose.

One way to clarify values is through the use of a values card sort or questionnaire. These tools present a list of common values, such as creativity, honesty, or adventure, and ask individuals to rank or select the values that resonate most deeply with them. By reflecting on the chosen values and exploring how they relate to one's life experiences and aspirations, individuals can gain a clearer sense of what gives their life meaning and purpose.

For Michael, who often feels like his sense of self is unstable and unpredictable, engaging in a values card sort is a revelatory experience. As he sorts through the cards, he realizes that his core values include compassion, growth, and contribution. These values resonate deeply with his desire to help others and make a positive difference in the world, even though he often feels like he's falling short. By setting specific goals related to his values, such as volunteering at a local community center or pursuing a degree in counseling, Michael begins to feel a greater sense of direction and stability in his life. Even on days when his sense of self feels shaky, he can anchor himself in his values and take small steps towards a life that feels meaningful and worthwhile.

A third strategy for developing a more stable and positive sense of self is to practice self-compassion and self-acceptance. Self-compassion involves treating oneself with kindness, understanding, and forgiveness, recognizing that all humans are imperfect and deserving of care. Self-acceptance involves embracing all aspects of oneself, including strengths, weaknesses, and everything in between, with a sense of openness and non-judgment.

For individuals with BPD, who often struggle with intense self-criticism and black-and-white thinking, practicing self-compassion and self-acceptance can be challenging but transformative. One way to cultivate these qualities is through the use of loving-kindness meditation or self-compassion exercises. These practices involve silently repeating phrases of goodwill and understanding towards oneself, such as "May I be kind to myself" or "I accept myself, flaws and all."

Emily, who often swings between extreme self-praise and self-loathing, finds self-compassion exercises to be a powerful tool for developing a more balanced and accepting self-image. Each day, she sets aside time to sit quietly and repeat phrases of self-compassion, such as "I am doing the best I can" or "I am worthy of love and respect, even when I make mistakes." At first, these phrases feel foreign and uncomfortable, but over time, Emily begins to internalize a greater sense of self-acceptance and self-forgiveness. When she encounters setbacks or failures, she is better able to respond with self-kindness and understanding, rather than harsh self-judgment. As a result, her sense of self becomes more stable and resilient, less dependent on external validation or perfectionistic standards.

Developing a more stable and positive sense of self is an ongoing process, one that requires patience, persistence, and a willingness to try new things. It's important for individuals with BPD to approach this process with a spirit of self-compassion and curiosity, recognizing that progress may be slow and non-linear. Setbacks and challenges are a normal part of the journey, not a sign of failure or inadequacy.

Seeking support from a therapist, particularly one trained in evidence-based treatments for BPD such as Dialectical Behavior Therapy (DBT) or Schema Therapy, can be invaluable in the process of developing a stronger sense of self. A skilled therapist can provide guidance, tools, and a safe space for self-exploration and skill-building, helping individuals navigate the complexities of identity development and self-discovery.

Ultimately, developing a more stable and positive sense of self is about more than just reducing symptoms or improving functioning.

It's about claiming one's inherent worth, dignity, and potential as a unique and valuable human being. By learning to know, accept, and direct oneself with greater clarity and compassion, individuals with BPD can build a life that feels authentic, meaningful, and fulfilling, even in the face of ongoing challenges and uncertainties.

Building self-esteem and self-confidence

Closely related to the development of a stable and positive sense of self is the building of self-esteem and self-confidence. Self-esteem refers to the overall sense of self-worth and self-respect that individuals hold about themselves, while self-confidence refers to the belief in one's abilities and capacity to succeed in specific situations. For individuals with BPD, who often struggle with chronic feelings of worthlessness, inadequacy, and self-doubt, building self-esteem and self-confidence is a crucial aspect of recovery and well-being.

One key strategy for building self-esteem is to challenge negative self-talk and cognitive distortions. Individuals with BPD often engage in harsh, self-critical inner dialogues, focusing on perceived flaws, mistakes, or shortcomings while discounting positive qualities and accomplishments. These negative thought patterns can become so habitual that they feel like unquestionable truths, contributing to a pervasive sense of low self-worth.

Cognitive restructuring techniques, such as those used in Cognitive Behavioral Therapy (CBT), can be powerful tools for challenging negative self-talk and developing a more balanced and compassionate inner dialogue. These techniques involve identifying automatic negative thoughts, examining the evidence for and against them, and generating alternative, more realistic and self-supportive thoughts.

For Sarah, who often tells herself that she's "stupid" or "unlovable," learning to catch and challenge these negative thoughts is a game-changer. With the help of her therapist, she begins to notice when she's engaging in self-critical inner talk and to question the validity of these thoughts. When she catches herself thinking "I'm so stupid," she asks herself, "Is this thought based on facts or feelings? What evidence do I have that I'm actually stupid?" By examining her thoughts more objectively, Sarah starts to recognize that her self-criticisms are often exaggerated or untrue. She learns to generate alternative, more self-compassionate thoughts, such as "I may have made a mistake, but that doesn't mean I'm stupid. I'm human, and I'm learning and growing every day." Over time, this practice of cognitive restructuring helps Sarah develop a more balanced and accepting relationship with herself, boosting her overall sense of self-esteem.

Another strategy for building self-esteem is to focus on strengths, accomplishments, and positive qualities. Individuals with BPD often have a bias towards noticing and dwelling on negative aspects of themselves and their lives, while overlooking or discounting positive aspects. This negative bias can contribute to a distorted and overly critical self-image, perpetuating feelings of worthlessness and inadequacy.

One way to counteract this negative bias is to intentionally culti-vate a strengths-based focus, regularly reflecting on and acknowl-edging one's positive qualities, skills, and achievements. This can involve keeping a daily gratitude journal, in which individuals write down three things they appreciate about themselves or their lives each day. It can also involve seeking out feedback from trusted others about one's strengths and contributions, or setting aside time for activities that showcase one's talents and abilities.

For Michael, who often feels like a failure despite his many accomplishments, learning to focus on his strengths is an ongoing practice. He starts keeping a "success journal," in which he writes down his daily achievements, no matter how small. Some days, his successes include things like "cooked a healthy meal" or "called a friend who needed support." Other days, they include larger accom-plishments, such as "finished a major project at work" or "ran a personal best time in a 5K race." By intentionally focusing on his strengths and successes, Michael starts to develop a more balanced and self-appreciative perspective. He begins to see himself not just as someone who struggles with BPD, but as a whole person with valuable qualities and contributions to offer.

Building self-confidence, or the belief in one's ability to succeed in specific situations, is another important aspect of developing a stronger sense of self. Self-confidence is often built through a combination of skill-building, goal-setting, and mastery experiences, in which individuals take on challenges and experience a sense of accomplishment and competence.

For individuals with BPD, who may struggle with self-doubt and a fear of failure, building self-confidence can involve starting with small, manageable goals and gradually working up to larger challenges. It can also involve breaking down larger goals into smaller, more achievable steps, and celebrating each step along the way.

Emily, who often feels overwhelmed and incapable when faced with new challenges, learns to build her self-confidence through a process of gradual exposure and skills-building. With the support of her therapist, she identifies a specific goal that feels important but intimidating, such as giving a presentation at work. She then breaks this goal down into smaller, more manageable steps, such as:

1 Outlining the presentation content

2 Practicing the presentation in front of a mirror

3 Practicing the presentation with a trusted friend or colleague

4 Rehearsing the presentation in the actual presentation space

5 Giving the presentation to a small, supportive group

6 Giving the presentation to a larger, more diverse audience

As Emily works through each step, she focuses on developing and applying specific skills, such as deep breathing, positive self-talk, and grounding techniques. She also makes sure to acknowledge and celebrate her progress along the way, recognizing that each step is a success in itself. By the time Emily gives her final presentation, she feels a sense of pride and accomplishment, having built her self-confidence through a process of gradual mastery and self-compassion.

Mindfulness and Acceptance: Incorporating Mindfulness Techniques into CBT for BPD

Mindfulness and acceptance are two powerful tools that can be integrated into Cognitive Behavioral Therapy (CBT) to help individuals with Borderline Personality Disorder (BPD) better manage their symptoms and improve their overall well-being. Mindfulness involves paying attention to the present moment with openness, curiosity, and non-judgment, while acceptance involves learning to embrace one's thoughts, feelings, and experiences without trying to change or suppress them. In this chapter, we will introduce the concept of mindfulness, explore its benefits for individuals with BPD, learn specific mindfulness techniques for reducing stress and increasing self-awareness, and discuss the importance of practicing acceptance and non-judgmental attitudes towards thoughts and emotions.

Introducing mindfulness and its benefits for BPD

Mindfulness is a practice that has its roots in ancient Buddhist traditions but has gained widespread popularity in recent years as a secular tool for stress reduction, emotional regulation, and personal growth. At its core, mindfulness is about being fully present and aware in the current moment, without getting caught up in worries about the past or fears about the future. It involves observing one's thoughts, feelings, and sensations with a sense of openness and curiosity, without trying to change or judge them.

For individuals with BPD, who often struggle with intense and rapidly shifting emotions, impulsivity, and a chronic sense of emptiness or disconnection, mindfulness can offer a powerful path towards greater stability, self-awareness, and emotional balance. By learning to anchor themselves in the present moment and observe their inner experiences with a sense of spaciousness and acceptance, individuals with BPD can develop a greater capacity to tolerate distress, regulate their emotions, and respond to life's challenges with flexibility and resilience.

Research has shown that incorporating mindfulness into CBT can be particularly effective for individuals with BPD. A study published in the Journal of Psychiatric Practice found that a mindfulness-based CBT program led to significant reductions in BPD symptoms, as well as improvements in mindfulness skills, emotional regulation, and interpersonal functioning (Feliu-Soler et al., 2014). Another study published in the journal Behaviour Research and Therapy found that a brief mindfulness intervention led to reductions in impulsivity and increases in self-control among individuals with BPD (Soler et al., 2016).

The benefits of mindfulness for individuals with BPD are numerous and far-reaching. One of the primary benefits is increased emotional awareness and clarity. By learning to observe their thoughts and feelings with a sense of curiosity and non-judgment, individuals with BPD can gain a clearer understanding of their emotional landscape and the triggers that contribute to their distress. This increased awareness can help them respond to their emotions with greater skill and intentionality, rather than getting swept away by intense and impulsive reactions.

For example, Sarah, who struggles with BPD, often finds herself feeling overwhelmed and reactive when her partner expresses disappointment or frustration with her. In the past, she would either lash out in anger or withdraw into a spiral of shame and self-loathing, leading to painful conflicts and disconnection in her relationship. Through mindfulness practice, Sarah learns to notice her thoughts and feelings as they arise in these moments, without getting hooked by them. She observes the sensations of tightness in her chest and the racing thoughts of "I'm a terrible partner" or "He's going to leave me," but rather than reacting impulsively, she takes a few deep breaths and reminds herself that these thoughts and feelings are temporary and do not define her. With practice, Sarah finds that she is able to respond to her partner's concerns with greater calm and clarity, leading to more productive conversations and a stronger sense of connection.

Another benefit of mindfulness for individuals with BPD is increased distress tolerance. One of the hallmarks of BPD is a difficulty tolerating uncomfortable or painful emotions, often leading to impulsive behaviors such as self-harm, substance abuse, or angry outbursts as a way to escape or numb the distress. Mindfulness teaches individuals to approach their discomfort with a sense of openness and acceptance, rather than avoidance or reactivity. By learning to sit with their painful emotions and observe them with a sense of curiosity and compassion, individuals with BPD can develop a greater capacity to ride out the waves of distress without getting pulled under.

Michael, who has struggled with BPD for many years, often finds himself turning to alcohol or self-injury when he feels over-whelmed by feelings of emptiness or abandonment. Through his mindfulness practice, he learns to notice these urges as they arise, without judging himself or acting on them impulsively. He practices bringing a sense of gentle attention to the sensations in his body, such as the tightness in his chest or the restlessness in his limbs, and observes them with a sense of openness and acceptance. He reminds himself that these feelings, no matter how painful, are temporary and will eventually pass. With time and practice, Michael finds that his ability to tolerate distress increases, and he is able to navigate his emotional landscape with greater resilience and skill.

Mindfulness can also help individuals with BPD cultivate a greater sense of self-awareness and self-compassion. Many individuals with BPD struggle with a harsh and unrelenting inner critic, constantly berating themselves for their perceived flaws and mistakes. This negative self-talk can fuel feelings of worthlessness, shame, and self-loathing, making it difficult to develop a stable and positive sense of self. Mindfulness invites individuals to observe their self-critical thoughts with a sense of distance and perspective, recognizing that they are not facts, but rather mental events that come and go like passing clouds.

Emily, who has struggled with low self-esteem and self-harm related to her BPD, often finds herself caught in a loop of negative self-talk, telling herself that she is "broken" or "unlovable." Through her mindfulness practice, she learns to catch these thoughts as they arise and to observe them with a sense of gentle curiosity. Rather than getting sucked into the content of the thoughts, she practices noticing them as mental events, saying to herself, "I'm having the thought that I'm broken" or "I'm noticing a feeling of worthlessness arising." This subtle shift in perspective helps Emily create a sense of space around her negative self-talk, reducing its power and intensity. She also practices bringing a sense of kindness and compassion to her own suffering, placing a hand on her heart and offering herself words of comfort and understanding. With practice, Emily finds that her inner critic softens, and she is able to relate to herself with greater warmth and acceptance.

Finally, mindfulness can help individuals with BPD improve their interpersonal relationships by cultivating greater empathy, compassion, and emotional attunement. Many individuals with BPD struggle with a phenomenon known as "empathy fatigue," in which they become so overwhelmed by the intensity of their own emotions that they have difficulty attuning to the feelings and needs of others. This can lead to conflicts, misunderstandings, and a sense of disconnection in relationships. Mindfulness helps individuals regulate their own emotional reactivity so that they can be more fully present and available to others.

Sarah, who often struggles to connect with her friends and family due to her intense mood swings and fear of abandonment, finds that mindfulness helps her show up in her relationships with greater stability and care. Before meeting up with a friend, she takes a few moments to ground herself in the present moment, noticing her breath and any sensations in her body. She sets an intention to listen deeply and to be fully present with her friend, without getting caught up in her own worries or insecurities. During the interaction, if she notices herself starting to feel overwhelmed or reactive, she takes a few deep breaths and returns her attention to the present moment. With practice, Sarah finds that she is able to engage in her relationships with greater ease and enjoyment, feeling more connected and attuned to the people in her life.

Incorporating mindfulness into CBT for BPD can help individuals develop a more balanced and accepting relationship with their thoughts, feelings, and experiences. By learning to anchor themselves in the present moment and observe their inner world with curiosity and compassion, individuals with BPD can reduce their emotional reactivity, increase their distress tolerance, and cultivate a greater sense of self-awareness and self-compassion. These skills, in turn, can lead to improved relationships, reduced impulsivity, and a greater overall sense of well-being and life satisfaction.

Learning mindfulness techniques for reducing stress and increasing self-awareness

While the concept of mindfulness may sound simple, practicing it effectively requires a set of specific skills and techniques that can be learned and cultivated over time. In this section, we will explore some of the core mindfulness techniques that can be incorporated into CBT for BPD, with a focus on reducing stress, increasing self-awareness, and promoting emotional regulation.

One of the foundational mindfulness techniques is the practice of mindful breathing. This involves bringing one's attention to the physical sensations of the breath, noticing the inhale and exhale without trying to change or control the breath in any way. By anchoring one's attention in the breath, individuals can cultivate a sense of present-moment awareness and reduce the pull of distressing thoughts and emotions.

To practice mindful breathing, find a comfortable seated position, either on a cushion or in a chair, with your back straight and your feet planted firmly on the ground. Close your eyes or soften your gaze, and begin to notice the physical sensations of your breath. You might notice the cool air entering your nostrils on the inhale, or the gentle rise and fall of your chest or belly. If your mind starts to wander, as it inevitably will, simply notice that it has wandered and gently redirect your attention back to the breath. You can silently say to yourself, "inhaling" on the inhale and "exhaling" on the exhale to help anchor your attention.

Emily, who often finds herself caught up in anxious thoughts and worries, finds that practicing mindful breathing helps her feel more grounded and centered. She sets aside 10 minutes each morning to sit quietly and focus on her breath, noticing any thoughts or sensations that arise without getting hooked by them. With practice, she finds that she is able to approach her day with a greater sense of calm and clarity, less likely to get overwhelmed by the stresses and challenges that come her way.

Another core mindfulness technique is the body scan. This involves systematically directing one's attention to different parts of the body, noticing any sensations that are present without trying to change them. The body scan can help individuals develop a greater sense of body awareness, as well as cultivate a more accepting and compassionate relationship with their physical experience.

To practice the body scan, lie down on your back in a comfortable position, with your arms at your sides and your legs extended. Close your eyes and take a few deep breaths, noticing the physical sensations of the breath. Then, bring your attention to your toes, noticing any sensations that are present, such as warmth, tingling, or pressure. Slowly move your attention up through your feet, ankles, calves, and knees, noticing any sensations that arise along the way. Continue moving your attention up through your thighs, hips, belly, chest, back, shoulders, arms, hands, neck, face, and head, taking your time to notice and acknowledge any sensations that are present. If your mind starts to wander, simply notice that it has wandered and gently redirect your attention back to the body.

Michael, who often struggles with feelings of numbness and disconnection related to his BPD, finds that practicing the body scan helps him feel more grounded and present in his physical experience. He sets aside 20 minutes each evening to lie down and scan through his body, noticing any areas of tension, discomfort, or ease. With practice, he finds that he is able to develop a greater sense of embodiment and self-awareness, feeling more connected to his physical experience and less caught up in his distressing thoughts and emotions.

Mindfulness can also be practiced through the technique of mindful observation. This involves bringing a sense of curious attention to one's surroundings, noticing the sights, sounds, smells, and sensations that are present in the moment. Mindful observation can help individuals develop a greater sense of presence and appreciation for the richness and complexity of their environment.

To practice mindful observation, choose an object or scene to focus on, such as a flower, a candle flame, or a landscape. Bring your full attention to the object, noticing its colors, shapes, textures, and any other sensory details that are present. If your mind starts to wander or get caught up in thoughts or judgments, simply notice that this has happened and gently redirect your attention back to the object. You can also expand your awareness to include any sounds, smells, or physical sensations that are present in the moment, such as the chirping of birds or the feeling of the sun on your skin.

Sarah, who often feels overwhelmed and disconnected from the world around her, finds that practicing mindful observation helps her feel more grounded and engaged with her environment. She sets aside a few minutes each day to step outside and simply observe the natural world around her, noticing the colors of the sky, the texture of the grass beneath her feet, and the sounds of the birds and insects. With practice, she finds that she is able to approach her daily life with a greater sense of presence and appreciation, less likely to get caught up in her own distressing thoughts and worries.

Another powerful mindfulness technique is the practice of loving-kindness or self-compassion. This involves directing thoughts and feelings of warmth, care, and understanding towards oneself and others. Loving-kindness practice can help individuals with BPD develop a more accepting and compassionate relationship with themselves, as well as cultivate greater empathy and connection with others.

To practice loving-kindness, find a comfortable seated position and take a few deep breaths, noticing the physical sensations of the breath. Then, bring to mind an image of yourself, or of someone else who is suffering. Silently repeat phrases of loving-kindness towards yourself or the other person, such as "May I be happy," "May I be healthy," "May I be safe," or "May I be at peace." Notice any feelings of warmth, care, or compassion that arise as you repeat these phrases. If your mind starts to wander or get caught up in judgments or criticisms, simply notice that this has happened and gently redirect your attention back to the phrases of loving-kindness.

Emily, who often struggles with intense self-criticism and shame related to her BPD, finds that practicing loving-kindness helps her develop a more accepting and compassionate relationship with herself. She sets aside a few minutes each day to silently repeat phrases of loving-kindness towards herself, such as "May I be kind to myself," "May I accept myself as I am," or "May I forgive myself for my mistakes." With practice, she finds that her inner critic begins to soften, and she is able to approach herself with greater warmth and understanding.

Finally, mindfulness can be incorporated into daily life through the practice of informal mindfulness. This involves bringing a sense of present-moment awareness and acceptance to one's everyday activities, such as eating, walking, or doing household chores. Informal mindfulness can help individuals with BPD cultivate a greater sense of presence and engagement in their daily lives, as well as reduce stress and increase overall well-being.

To practice informal mindfulness, choose an activity that you typically do on autopilot, such as brushing your teeth, washing the dishes, or driving to work. As you engage in the activity, bring your full attention to the sensory details of the experience, such as the taste of the toothpaste, the feeling of the warm water on your hands, or the sensation of the steering wheel beneath your fingers. If your mind starts to wander or get caught up in thoughts or worries, simply notice that this has happened and gently redirect your attention back to the activity at hand.

Michael, who often feels disconnected and numb in his daily life, finds that practicing informal mindfulness helps him feel more engaged and present in his everyday experiences. He sets an intention to bring mindful awareness to one activity each day, such as eating his lunch or taking a shower. As he engages in the activity, he notices the sensory details of the experience, such as the taste and texture of his food, or the feeling of the warm water on his skin. With practice, he finds that he is able to approach his daily life with a greater sense of vitality and appreciation, less likely to get caught up in his own distressing thoughts and emotions.

Practicing acceptance and non-judgmental attitudes towards thoughts and emotions

In addition to the specific mindfulness techniques described above, a key component of incorporating mindfulness into CBT for BPD is the cultivation of acceptance and non-judgmental attitudes towards one's thoughts and emotions. Acceptance involves learning to embrace one's inner experiences, whether pleasant or painful, without trying to change, suppress, or avoid them. Non-judgmental awareness involves observing one's thoughts and feelings with a sense of openness and curiosity, without getting caught up in evaluations of "good" or "bad," "right" or "wrong."

For individuals with BPD, who often struggle with intense and rapidly shifting emotions, as well as a deep sense of self-criticism and shame, practicing acceptance and non-judgment can be particularly challenging. There may be a strong urge to push away or numb painful feelings, or to get caught up in self-critical thoughts and judgments. However, research has shown that attempts to suppress or avoid emotions can actually increase their intensity and frequency over time, leading to a vicious cycle of emotional reactivity and distress.

In contrast, practicing acceptance and non-judgment allows individuals to develop a more balanced and flexible relationship with their inner experiences. By learning to observe their thoughts and feelings with a sense of openness and curiosity, individuals can gain a greater understanding of their emotional landscape.

8

Coping with Impulsivity and Self-Destructive Behaviors: Techniques for Behavioral Modification

Impulsivity and self-destructive behaviors are common challenges faced by individuals with Borderline Personality Disorder (BPD). These behaviors can range from reckless driving, excessive spending, and substance abuse to self-harm, disordered eating, and suicidal gestures. While these behaviors may provide temporary relief from distressing emotions or thoughts, they ultimately lead to negative consequences and perpetuate a cycle of shame, guilt, and emotional dysregulation. In this chapter, we will explore strategies for identifying impulsive and self-destructive behaviors, learning techniques for managing urges and impulses, and developing alternative coping mechanisms and positive behaviors.

Identifying impulsive and self-destructive behaviors

The first step in addressing impulsive and self-destructive behaviors is to develop a clear understanding of what these behaviors look like and how they manifest in one's life. Impulsive behaviors are characterized by a lack of forethought or consideration of consequences, often driven by a strong urge or desire for immediate gratification. Self-destructive behaviors, on the other hand, are those that cause harm to oneself, whether physical, emotional, or social.

Some common examples of impulsive behaviors in individuals with BPD include:

1. Reckless driving, such as speeding, running red lights, or driving under the influence

2. Impulsive spending, leading to financial strain or debt

3. Risky sexual behaviors, such as unprotected sex with multiple partners

4. Substance abuse, including alcohol, drugs, or prescription medications

5. Binge eating or purging

6. Angry outbursts or aggressive behavior towards others

7. Abruptly quitting a job or ending a relationship

Self-destructive behaviors, which often overlap with impulsive behaviors, may include:

1. Cutting, burning, or otherwise injuring oneself

2. Picking at skin or interfering with wound healing

3. Engaging in dangerous or life-threatening activities

4. Neglecting physical health, such as not eating or sleeping properly

5. Sabotaging relationships or opportunities for success

6. Attempting suicide or making suicidal gestures

It's important to note that not all individuals with BPD will engage in all of these behaviors, and the severity and frequency of these behaviors can vary widely from person to person. However, the presence of impulsive and self-destructive behaviors is a common feature of BPD and can cause significant distress and impairment in daily functioning.

One reason why identifying these behaviors is so important is that they often serve as maladaptive coping mechanisms for dealing with intense emotions or distressing thoughts. For individuals with BPD, who often experience emotions more intensely and have difficulty regulating them, impulsive and self-destructive behaviors may provide a sense of relief, control, or distraction from inner turmoil. Understanding the function that these behaviors serve is crucial for developing more effective and adaptive coping strategies.

For example, Sarah, who struggles with BPD, finds that whenever she experiences feelings of abandonment or rejection, she has a strong urge to engage in self-harm. Cutting her skin provides a temporary sense of relief and numbness from the overwhelming emotions she is experiencing. However, this relief is short-lived, and Sarah is left with feelings of shame, guilt, and physical pain. By identifying this pattern and understanding the function that self-harm serves for her, Sarah can begin to explore alternative coping strategies that address her emotional needs in a healthier way.

Another reason why identifying impulsive and self-destructive behaviors is important is that these behaviors can have serious negative consequences for individuals with BPD and those around them. Reckless driving, for example, puts oneself and others at risk of physical harm or legal consequences. Impulsive spending can lead to financial instability and stress. Substance abuse can have detrimental effects on physical and mental health, as well as relationships and employment. Self-harm and suicidal behaviors can result in serious injury, hospitalization, or even death.

Moreover, engaging in impulsive and self-destructive behaviors can perpetuate a cycle of shame, guilt, and self-loathing. Individuals with BPD may feel a sense of shame or disappointment in themselves for engaging in these behaviors, leading to negative self-talk and a worsening of symptoms. This, in turn, can increase the likelihood of turning to these behaviors again in the future as a way to cope with the intensified emotions.

Michael, who has struggled with BPD for many years, has a history of impulsive aggression towards his partners. Whenever he feels criticized or misunderstood, he lashes out with hurtful words or even physical violence. Afterwards, he is flooded with feelings of remorse, self-hatred, and fear of abandonment, which only intensify his urges to lash out again in the future. By recognizing this cycle and the negative impact it has on his relationships and self-esteem, Michael can begin to break the pattern and learn healthier ways of communicating his needs and emotions.

Identifying impulsive and self-destructive behaviors is a crucial first step in the process of change. By bringing awareness to these patterns and understanding their function and consequences, individuals with BPD can begin to develop the motivation and skills needed to make positive changes in their lives. Working with a therapist who is trained in CBT for BPD can provide a safe and supportive space for exploring these behaviors and developing a plan for change.

Learning strategies for managing urges and impulses

Once impulsive and self-destructive behaviors have been identified, the next step is to develop strategies for managing the urges and impulses that drive these behaviors. While it may not be possible to eliminate urges and impulses entirely, individuals with BPD can learn skills for tolerating distress, regulating emotions, and making healthier choices in the face of intense desires.

One effective strategy for managing urges and impulses is urge surfing. This technique, which is rooted in mindfulness practices, involves observing and "riding out" urges or cravings without acting on them. The idea behind urge surfing is that urges, like waves in the ocean, will naturally rise, peak, and eventually subside on their own if not fueled by attention or action.

To practice urge surfing, start by identifying the physical sensations associated with the urge, such as tightness in the chest, a racing heartbeat, or a sense of restlessness. Take a few deep breaths and bring your attention to these sensations, observing them with curiosity and without judgment. Notice any thoughts or emotions that arise in response to the urge, but try not to get caught up in them. Instead, imagine yourself as a surfer riding the wave of the urge, staying present and balanced as it rises and falls. With practice, you may find that the intensity of the urge gradually decreases, and you are able to let it pass without acting on it.

Sarah, who struggles with urges to self-harm, finds urge surfing to be a helpful tool for managing these impulses. When she notices the familiar sensation of tension and a strong desire to cut herself, she takes a few deep breaths and focuses her attention on the physical sensations in her body. She imagines the urge as a wave that she is riding, observing its intensity without getting swept up in it. As she continues to breathe and stay present, Sarah notices that the urge begins to subside on its own, and she is able to let it pass without engaging in self-harm.

Another strategy for managing urges and impulses is to create a delay between the urge and the behavior. Often, impulsive behaviors are driven by a sense of urgency or a desire for immediate relief. By introducing a delay or pause before acting on an urge, individuals with BPD can create space for reflection and consider alternative actions.

One way to create a delay is to set a specific time limit for waiting before engaging in the behavior. For example, if you have an urge to binge eat, you might set a timer for 20 minutes and commit to waiting until the timer goes off before deciding whether to act on the urge. During this waiting period, you can engage in alternative activities, such as taking a walk, calling a friend, or practicing a relaxation technique. By the time the timer goes off, the intensity of the urge may have decreased, and you may be able to make a more mindful choice.

Michael, who struggles with impulsive spending, uses the delay strategy to help manage his urges to buy things he doesn't need. Whenever he feels the impulse to make a purchase, he commits to waiting at least 24 hours before buying anything. During this delay period, he asks himself questions like, "Do I really need this item? How will I feel about this purchase tomorrow? Is there something else I could do with this money that would be more aligned with my goals?" By creating space for reflection and considering the long-term consequences of his actions, Michael is often able to make more intentional choices with his money.

Distraction is another useful strategy for managing urges and impulses. When individuals with BPD are caught up in an intense urge, it can be difficult to think clearly or consider alternative actions. By shifting attention to a different activity or stimulus, the power of the urge can be reduced, making it easier to resist acting on it.

Distraction techniques can include a wide range of activities, such as:

1. Engaging in physical exercise or movement

2. Listening to music or a podcast

3. Doing a puzzle or playing a game

4. Calling a friend or loved one for support

5. Cleaning or organizing one's space

6. Engaging in a creative hobby, such as drawing, writing, or playing an instrument

The key is to choose an activity that is enjoyable, engaging, and not harmful in itself. It's also important to have a list of distraction techniques readily available, so that when an urge arises, you have options to choose from rather than having to come up with ideas in the moment.

Emily, who struggles with urges to engage in risky sexual behaviors, finds that distraction is a helpful tool for managing these impulses. When she feels the desire to seek out a new sexual partner or engage in unprotected sex, she redirects her attention to a different activity, such as going for a run or working on a craft project. By immersing herself in a different sensory experience, Emily finds that the intensity of the sexual urge decreases, and she is able to make more mindful choices about her behavior.

Developing alternative coping mechanisms and positive behaviors

While managing urges and impulses is an important skill for individuals with BPD, it is equally important to develop alternative coping mechanisms and positive behaviors that can replace impulsive and self-destructive ones. By building a repertoire of healthy coping strategies and engaging in behaviors that promote well-being and self-care, individuals with BPD can improve their overall quality of life and reduce their reliance on maladaptive behaviors.

One key alternative coping mechanism is emotional regulation skills. As discussed in previous chapters, individuals with BPD often experience intense and rapidly shifting emotions that can be difficult to manage. By learning and practicing specific skills for regulating emotions, such as deep breathing, progressive muscle relaxation, or mindfulness techniques, individuals can reduce the intensity and duration of distressing emotions and decrease the urge to engage in impulsive or self-destructive behaviors.

For example, when Sarah feels overwhelmed by feelings of emptiness and abandonment, rather than turning to self-harm, she practices a grounding technique that helps her feel more centered and in control. She focuses on identifying five things she can see, four things she can touch, three things she can hear, two things she can smell, and one thing she can taste. By engaging her senses and anchoring herself in the present moment, Sarah finds that the intensity of her emotions decreases, and she is better able to tolerate the distress without resorting to self-harm.

Another important alternative coping mechanism is self-soothing. Self-soothing involves engaging in activities that promote a sense of comfort, safety, and well-being. These activities can be sensory in nature, such as taking a warm bath, wrapping oneself in a soft blanket, or listening to calming music. They can also involve positive self-talk, such as repeating affirmations or reminding oneself of one's strengths and accomplishments.

When Michael feels the urge to lash out at his partner during a conflict, he excuses himself and goes to a quiet room to practice self-soothing. He sits in a comfortable chair, closes his eyes, and focuses on taking slow, deep breaths. He visualizes a peaceful scene, such as a beach or a forest, and imagines himself feeling calm and grounded. Michael also repeats a soothing phrase to himself, such as "I am safe" or "I can handle this." By taking a break to soothe himself, Michael is able to return to the conversation with his partner in a more regulated and constructive state.

Developing positive behaviors is another crucial aspect of replacing impulsive and self-destructive ones. Positive behaviors are those that promote health, well-being, and a sense of accomplishment or enjoyment. These can include activities such as regular exercise, healthy eating, pursuing hobbies or interests, volunteering, or spending quality time with loved ones.

When Emily feels the urge to engage in risky sexual behaviors, she redirects her energy towards positive activities that make her feel good about herself. She joins a dance class, which provides her with a sense of community and an outlet for physical expression. She also starts volunteering at a local animal shelter, which gives her a sense of purpose and fulfillment. By investing her time and energy in activities that are meaningful and rewarding, Emily finds that her urges to engage in self-destructive behaviors decrease over time.

It's important to note that developing alternative coping mechanisms and positive behaviors is a gradual process that requires practice and patience. It may take time to identify which strategies work best for each individual, and there may be setbacks along the way. However, with consistent effort and support from a therapist or loved ones, individuals with BPD can build a foundation of healthy coping skills that promote resilience and well-being.

In addition to individual skill-building, it can also be helpful to address environmental factors that may trigger or reinforce impulsive and self-destructive behaviors. This might involve making changes to one's living situation, social circle, or daily routines to reduce exposure to high-risk situations or influences. It may also involve seeking out additional support or resources, such as joining a support group or participating in a structured treatment program.

Ultimately, the goal of developing alternative coping mechanisms and positive behaviors is to create a life that is rich, meaningful, and fulfilling, rather than one that is dominated by impulsivity and self-destruction. By learning to manage urges and impulses, regulate emotions, and engage in activities that promote well-being, individuals with BPD can build a strong foundation for recovery and growth.

In conclusion, impulsivity and self-destructive behaviors are common challenges faced by individuals with Borderline Personality Disorder, but they are not inevitable or untreatable. By learning to identify these behaviors and understand their functions and consequences, individuals with BPD can begin to develop the awareness and motivation needed for change.

Through strategies such as urge surfing, delaying, distraction, and emotional regulation skills, individuals can learn to manage the intense urges and impulses that drive these behaviors. By developing alternative coping mechanisms, such as self-soothing and positive behaviors, they can begin to replace maladaptive patterns with healthier ones that promote well-being and resilience.

It's important to approach this process with self-compassion and a willingness to seek support. Overcoming impulsive and self-destructive behaviors is a journey that requires patience, practice, and often the guidance of a trained therapist who can provide tools and support along the way.

Ultimately, the goal is not just to eliminate problematic behaviors, but to build a life that is rich, meaningful, and worth living. By developing a repertoire of healthy coping skills and engaging in activities that promote a sense of accomplishment, enjoyment, and connection, individuals with BPD can create a foundation for lasting recovery and personal growth.

With commitment, support, and a willingness to try new things, it is possible to break free from the cycle of impulsivity and self-destruction and build a life that reflects one's deepest values and aspirations. While the journey may be challenging at times, the destination - a life of greater stability, resilience, and fulfillment - is well worth the effort.

9

Preventing and Managing Crisis Situations: Safety Planning and Seeking Support

For individuals with Borderline Personality Disorder (BPD), crisis situations can be a frequent and distressing part of life. These crises may involve intense emotional distress, impulsive or self-destructive behaviors, or even thoughts of suicide. While it's not always possible to prevent crises from occurring, having a well-developed plan for managing them can help reduce their impact and duration, as well as increase a sense of safety and control. In this chapter, we will explore strategies for recognizing warning signs of a potential crisis, creating a personalized safety plan, and identifying support systems and resources for crisis management.

Recognizing warning signs of a potential crisis

The first step in preventing and managing crisis situations is to become attuned to the warning signs that a crisis may be developing. These warning signs can be different for each individual, but often involve a combination of emotional, cognitive, and behavioral changes that signal a worsening of symptoms or an increased risk of harmful behaviors.

Some common warning signs of a potential crisis in individuals with BPD include:

1. Intense and persistent feelings of anger, sadness, anxiety, or despair

2. Feelings of emptiness, numbness, or dissociation

3. Increased impulsivity or risk-taking behaviors

4. Urges to self-harm or engage in other self-destructive behaviors

5. Thoughts of suicide or feeling like life is not worth living

6. Withdrawal from friends, family, or usual activities

7. Neglecting self-care, such as not eating, sleeping, or attending to basic hygiene

8. Increased interpersonal conflicts or a sense of disconnection from others

9. Feeling overwhelmed, trapped, or unable to cope with life stressors

It's important to note that these warning signs may not always be apparent to others, as individuals with BPD may become skilled at masking their distress or presenting a facade of coping. This is why it's crucial for individuals to develop a keen awareness of their own unique warning signs and to communicate these to trusted loved ones or mental health professionals who can offer support.

One way to increase awareness of warning signs is to keep a mood and behavior journal. This involves tracking daily emotions, thoughts, and actions, as well as noting any triggering events or stressors. Over time, patterns may emerge that help individuals identify the early signs of a potential crisis, such as a sustained period of low mood, an increase in negative self-talk, or a tendency to isolate from others.

Sarah, who has struggled with BPD for many years, has learned to recognize her own warning signs through keeping a daily journal. She notices that before a crisis, she often experiences a period of intense anger and irritability, coupled with a strong urge to self-harm. She also tends to cancel plans with friends and neglect her self-care routine. By catching these warning signs early, Sarah can take proactive steps to prevent a full-blown crisis, such as reaching out for support, practicing her coping skills, or adjusting her self-care routine.

Another way to recognize warning signs is to involve loved ones or mental health professionals in the process. Sometimes, others may notice changes in an individual's mood or behavior before the individual themselves. By having open and honest conversations about what to look out for, and giving permission for others to express concern, individuals with BPD can create a safety net of support that can intervene early when a crisis is brewing.

Michael, who has a history of impulsive behaviors and suicide attempts, has given his therapist and his sister permission to check in with him if they notice any concerning changes. He has shared with them his personal warning signs, which include giving away possessions, making cryptic or hopeless statements, and withdrawing from all social contact. By having this open line of communication, Michael's support system can take swift action if they notice these warning signs, such as contacting his therapist, removing any dangerous items from his home, or even calling emergency services if needed.

It's important to remember that recognizing warning signs is not always straightforward, and there may be times when a crisis occurs without any apparent buildup. This is why having a comprehensive safety plan in place is essential, regardless of whether warning signs are present or not. However, by increasing awareness of personal triggers and patterns, individuals with BPD can be better equipped to prevent crises when possible, and to manage them more effectively when they do occur.

Creating a personalized safety plan

A safety plan is a written document that outlines a clear course of action for managing a crisis situation. It is created in advance, when the individual is in a stable state of mind, and can be relied upon during times of distress when clear thinking and decision-making may be impaired. A well-crafted safety plan is personalized to the individual's unique needs, triggers, and coping strategies, and involves input from both the individual and their support system.

The components of a safety plan may vary, but often include the following:

1. A list of personal warning signs that a crisis may be developing

2. Coping strategies and activities that can help reduce distress and promote a sense of calm

3. Contact information for supportive friends, family members, or professionals who can be reached out to in a crisis

4. Information about local crisis resources, such as hotlines, walk-in clinics, or emergency services

5. Reminders of reasons for living and personal strengths or accomplishments

6. Instructions for making the environment safe, such as removing access to means of self-harm or suicide

7. A clear plan for what to do if coping strategies are not working and professional intervention is needed

Creating a safety plan involves a process of self-reflection and collaboration. The individual must take time to consider what has helped them cope with crises in the past, as well as what has been less effective. They may need to brainstorm new strategies or ideas with the help of a therapist or loved one. The plan should be realistic and achievable, taking into account the individual's current resources and limitations.

Emily, who struggles with frequent suicidal ideation, works with her therapist to create a comprehensive safety plan. Together, they identify her warning signs, which include giving away personal possessions, writing farewell notes, and stockpiling medications. They also list her most effective coping strategies, such as calling her best friend, going for a walk in nature, or listening to a specific playlist of uplifting songs. Emily's plan includes the contact information for her therapist, her psychiatrist, and a local crisis hotline. She also lists her personal reasons for living, which include her love for her dog, her desire to finish her degree, and her belief in her own resilience. With the help of her therapist, Emily makes a plan to remove any dangerous items from her home and to give her medications to a trusted friend to hold onto. She also outlines a clear plan for what to do if her suicidal thoughts become overwhelming, which includes calling her therapist, going to the local emergency room, or calling 911 if needed.

Once a safety plan is created, it's important to review and update it regularly. Life circumstances, coping strategies, and support systems may change over time, so the plan must be adapted to remain relevant and effective. It's also crucial to share the plan with trusted loved ones or professionals who can help implement it during a crisis. This may involve giving copies of the plan to family members, close friends, or healthcare providers, as well as discussing the plan in detail so that everyone knows their role and what to do in an emergency.

It can be helpful to think of the safety plan as a living document, one that grows and changes with the individual over time. As new coping strategies are learned or new resources become available, these can be added to the plan. Similarly, if certain strategies are found to be ineffective or even triggering, they can be removed or adjusted. The goal is to have a plan that is comprehensive, yet flexible, and that provides a clear roadmap for navigating even the most challenging of crisis situations.

Identifying support systems and resources for crisis management

In addition to creating a personalized safety plan, identifying and accessing support systems and resources is a crucial component of crisis management for individuals with BPD. No one should have to face a crisis alone, and having a strong network of support can make all the difference in getting through difficult times.

Support systems can include a wide range of individuals and resources, such as:

1. Family members and close friends who are understanding and reliable

2. Mental health professionals, such as therapists, psychiatrists, or case managers

3. Support groups, either online or in-person, for individuals with BPD or related conditions

4. Crisis hotlines or textlines, which provide 24/7 support and resources

5. Religious or spiritual advisors, if this is an important part of the individual's life

6. Peer support specialists, who have personal experience with mental health challenges and can offer guidance and encouragement

7. Advocacy organizations, which can provide information, referrals, and support for individuals with BPD and their loved ones

When identifying support systems, it's important to consider not just who is available, but also who is truly supportive and understanding. Not everyone may have the knowledge, skills, or emotional capacity to provide effective support during a crisis. It's okay to be selective and to set boundaries around who is included in the support network.

Sarah, who has a large family and social circle, takes time to reflect on who in her life is most supportive and reliable. She identifies her sister, her best friend from college, and a cousin who also struggles with mental health issues as her core support system. She reaches out to these individuals and asks if they would be willing to be part of her crisis management plan. Together, they discuss what this would involve, such as being available for phone calls or texts, providing a safe space to stay if needed, or accompanying Sarah to appointments or the emergency room. Sarah also makes sure to express her gratitude for their support and to discuss how she can reciprocate and be there for them in times of need.

In addition to personal support systems, professional resources can be invaluable during a crisis. Mental health professionals, such as therapists or psychiatrists, can provide guidance, support, and interventions that are tailored to the individual's specific needs. They can also help coordinate care and make referrals to additional resources as needed.

Michael, who has been working with a therapist for several months, makes sure to include his therapist's contact information in his safety plan. He also asks his therapist for recommendations on local support groups or crisis resources. His therapist helps him locate a BPD support group that meets weekly at a community center, as well as a crisis hotline that is staffed by trained professionals. Michael attends a few support group meetings and finds that he feels less alone and more understood by others who have similar struggles. He also programs the crisis hotline number into his phone and makes a commitment to himself to call if he ever feels overwhelmed or in danger.

Online resources can also be a valuable addition to a crisis management plan. There are many websites, forums, and social media groups dedicated to providing support and information for individuals with BPD and their loved ones. These can be accessed 24/7 from anywhere with an internet connection, and can provide a sense of community and understanding that may be lacking in an individual's immediate environment.

Emily, who lives in a small town with limited mental health resources, finds solace in an online BPD support group. She is able to connect with others who understand her struggles and share coping strategies and resources. She also discovers a wealth of information on BPD and CBT through reputable websites such as the National Education Alliance for Borderline Personality Disorder (NEA-BPD) and the Linehan Institute. These resources help her feel more empowered and knowledgeable about her condition, and provide her with tools for managing her symptoms and communicating with her healthcare providers.

It's important to note that while support systems and resources are crucial, they are not a substitute for professional treatment. Crisis management is just one component of a comprehensive approach to treating BPD, which may also include individual therapy, group therapy, medication management, and skills training. The goal of crisis management is to provide immediate support and stabilization, but ongoing treatment is necessary for long-term recovery and wellbeing.

It's also important to recognize that accessing support and resources can be challenging, especially during a crisis. Stigma, financial barriers, or lack of availability can all make it difficult to get the help that is needed. This is why it's so important to have a plan in place before a crisis occurs, and to advocate for oneself and others in seeking out and securing necessary support.

Finally, it's essential to remember that seeking help is a sign of strength, not weakness. It takes courage and resilience to reach out for support, especially when struggling with intense emotions and distressing symptoms. By building a strong network of support and knowing how to access resources when needed, individuals with BPD can empower themselves to navigate even the most challenging of circumstances.

In conclusion, preventing and managing crisis situations is a critical component of treatment for Borderline Personality Disorder. By recognizing warning signs, creating a personalized safety plan, and identifying support systems and resources, individuals with BPD can increase their sense of safety, control, and resilience in the face of distressing symptoms and life stressors.

The process of crisis management is ongoing and requires regular review and updating as life circumstances and needs change. It involves a collaborative effort between the individual, their loved ones, and their healthcare providers to create a comprehensive and individualized plan for navigating difficult times.

Central to this process is a foundation of self-awareness, self-compassion, and a willingness to reach out for help. Recognizing one's own unique warning signs, triggers, and coping strategies is key to preventing crises when possible and managing them effectively when they do occur. Treating oneself with kindness and understanding, rather than judgment or criticism, can foster a sense of resilience and hope even in the darkest of moments.

Building a strong support system is also essential. This may involve cultivating relationships with friends and family members who are understanding and reliable, as well as identifying professional resources such as therapists, support groups, or crisis services. Knowing that one is not alone and that help is available can provide a lifeline during times of crisis.

Ultimately, the goal of crisis management is not just to survive, but to thrive. By developing a repertoire of skills, strategies, and supports for navigating difficult times, individuals with BPD can build a life that is rich, meaningful, and worth living. While the journey may be challenging at times, with the right tools and support, recovery and resilience are within reach.

It's important to remember that crisis situations, while distressing, are also opportunities for growth and learning. Each crisis navigated is a testament to an individual's strength and resourcefulness, and can serve as a foundation for future coping and resilience. By approaching crisis management with a spirit of curiosity, rather than fear, individuals with BPD can learn more about themselves and what they need to heal and grow.

This journey is not one that has to be taken alone. Seeking support, whether from loved ones, professionals, or peers, is a sign of wisdom and self-care. By reaching out and building connections, individuals with BPD can create a network of support that can sustain them through even the most trying of times.

Ultimately, preventing and managing crisis situations is about more than just survival - it's about reclaiming a sense of agency, empowerment, and hope in the face of significant challenges. With the right skills, strategies, and support, individuals with BPD can navigate crises with greater ease and confidence, and move towards a life of lasting wellbeing and fulfillment. The path may not always be easy, but it is one worth taking, step by step, day by day, with courage and commitment.

10

Maintaining Progress and Preventing Relapse: Strategies for Long-Term Success with CBT

Cognitive Behavioral Therapy (CBT) can be a highly effective treatment for Borderline Personality Disorder (BPD), offering individuals a wide range of skills and strategies for managing their symptoms, improving their relationships, and enhancing their overall quality of life. However, the journey of recovery is not always a straight line, and even after making significant progress in therapy, individuals with BPD may encounter challenges, setbacks, or relapses along the way. In this final chapter, we will explore strategies for maintaining the progress made in CBT, preventing relapse, and ensuring long-term success. We will discuss the importance of consolidating skills learned throughout therapy, developing a relapse prevention plan, and establishing a support network and continuing self-care practices.

Consolidating skills learned throughout therapy

One of the key factors in maintaining progress after CBT is the ongoing practice and application of the skills learned throughout therapy. CBT is not just about gaining insight or understanding, but about developing practical, actionable strategies for managing thoughts, emotions, and behaviors in real-world situations. As such, the skills learned in therapy must be consistently practiced and integrated into daily life in order to be effective long-term.

Some of the core skills that are often addressed in CBT for BPD include:

1. Mindfulness: Learning to be present and non-judgmental in the moment, observing thoughts and emotions without getting caught up in them.

2. Emotion regulation: Developing strategies for managing intense emotions, such as deep breathing, progressive muscle relaxation, or visualizations.

3. Distress tolerance: Building the capacity to withstand and cope with difficult or uncomfortable emotions without resorting to harmful behaviors.

4. Interpersonal effectiveness: Learning to communicate needs, set boundaries, and navigate relationships in a healthy and assertive way.

5. Cognitive restructuring: Identifying and challenging unhelpful or distorted thoughts, and replacing them with more balanced and realistic perspectives.

While these skills may be introduced and practiced within the context of therapy sessions, the real work of consolidation happens outside of the therapy room. Individuals must make a conscious effort to apply these skills in their daily lives, even when not in crisis or distress. This involves a commitment to ongoing practice, even when it feels difficult or uncomfortable.

One way to support skill consolidation is to create a regular practice schedule. This might involve setting aside specific times each day or week to practice mindfulness, emotion regulation, or interpersonal skills. It can be helpful to tie these practices to existing routines or habits, such as practicing deep breathing each morning upon waking, or reviewing cognitive restructuring exercises each night before bed.

Sarah, who has completed a course of CBT for BPD, makes a commitment to practicing her skills every day. She sets a reminder on her phone to practice mindfulness for 10 minutes each morning, focusing on her breath and observing her thoughts and emotions without judgment. She also schedules weekly check-ins with herself to review her emotion regulation and distress tolerance skills, identifying any challenging situations that arose during the week and reflecting on how she coped. By making skill practice a regular part of her routine, Sarah is able to keep the lessons of CBT fresh in her mind and integrate them more fully into her life.

Another way to consolidate skills is to seek out opportunities to apply them in real-world situations. This might involve intentionally engaging in activities or interactions that are challenging or triggering, with the goal of practicing new coping strategies. It can also involve reflecting on past experiences and considering how skills could have been applied, or how they might be applied in similar situations in the future.

Michael, who struggles with intense anger and impulsivity, makes a point of practicing his interpersonal effectiveness skills in his daily interactions. When he finds himself in a frustrating situation, such as a long line at the grocery store or a miscommunication with a coworker, he takes a moment to pause and consider how he wants to respond. He practices assertive communication, expressing his needs or concerns clearly and calmly, rather than lashing out or shutting down. He also practices active listening, making an effort to understand the other person's perspective before reacting. By consciously applying his skills in these everyday moments, Michael is able to strengthen his ability to handle conflicts and maintain healthy relationships.

It's important to recognize that skill consolidation is an ongoing process, not a one-time event. Even after completing a course of CBT, individuals may need to continue practicing and refining their skills over time. Life circumstances, stressors, and triggers may change, requiring adaptation and flexibility in the application of skills. It's also normal to have setbacks or lapses in skill use, especially during times of high stress or transition. The key is to approach these moments with self-compassion and a commitment to getting back on track, rather than self-criticism or abandonment of skills altogether.

In addition to personal practice, ongoing support from a therapist or therapy group can be invaluable in consolidating skills. Many individuals find it helpful to continue attending therapy sessions on a maintenance basis, even after the initial course of treatment is complete. This provides a space for accountability, feedback, and fine-tuning of skills, as well as support during challenging times. Some individuals may also benefit from joining a skills-based support group, such as Dialectical Behavior Therapy (DBT) skills training group, to reinforce and expand their skill set.

Emily, who has a history of self-harm and suicidal ideation, continues to attend individual therapy sessions once a month after completing a course of CBT. She finds that these sessions provide a valuable space for her to check in on her progress, troubleshoot any challenges that have arisen, and set goals for ongoing skill practice. She also joins a local DBT skills group, which meets weekly to review and practice core skills such as mindfulness, emotion regulation, and distress tolerance. By staying engaged in ongoing support and skill-building, Emily is able to maintain her progress and continue growing in her recovery.

Ultimately, the consolidation of skills learned in CBT is a personal responsibility that requires ongoing commitment, practice, and self-reflection. By making skill use a regular part of daily life, seeking out opportunities for real-world application, and engaging in ongoing support and skill-building, individuals with BPD can ensure that the gains made in therapy are sustained and strengthened over time. This lays the foundation for long-term success and resilience in the face of life's challenges.

Developing a relapse prevention plan

Another key strategy for maintaining progress after CBT is the development of a relapse prevention plan. A relapse prevention plan is a proactive strategy for identifying and managing potential triggers, warning signs, and high-risk situations that could lead to a recurrence of symptoms or a return to unhealthy patterns of behavior. By anticipating these challenges and developing a concrete plan for coping with them, individuals can reduce the risk of relapse and maintain their hard-won progress.

The first step in developing a relapse prevention plan is to identify personal triggers and warning signs. Triggers are the people, places, situations, or experiences that tend to provoke distressing emotions, thoughts, or urges. Warning signs are the internal experiences or behavioral changes that indicate that an individual may be moving towards a relapse. These can be different for everyone, but some common examples include:

Triggers:
- Interpersonal conflicts or rejections
- Stressful life events, such as job loss or financial strain
- Exposure to trauma reminders or other distressing stimuli
- Substance use or other risky behaviors

Warning Signs:
- Increased feelings of anxiety, sadness, anger, or emptiness
- Disruptions in sleep or appetite
- Isolating from friends or activities
- Neglecting self-care or responsibilities
- Increased self-critical thoughts or urges to self-harm

Once triggers and warning signs have been identified, the next step is to develop a plan for managing them. This plan should include specific coping strategies, supports, and resources that can be accessed in times of need. It's important that this plan is concrete, detailed, and realistic, taking into account the individual's unique circumstances and preferences.

Some components of a relapse prevention plan might include:

1. A list of healthy coping strategies, such as deep breathing, meditation, journaling, art, or exercise, that can be used to manage distressing emotions and thoughts.

2. A support network of trusted friends, family members, or professionals who can be contacted for help or encouragement during difficult times. This should include specific names, phone numbers, and instructions for reaching out.

3. A safe place, such as a park, library, or friend's house, where the individual can go to regroup and practice self-care when feeling triggered or overwhelmed.

4. A list of positive affirmations, reminders, or inspiring quotes that can serve as encouragement and motivation.

5. A schedule of regular self-care activities, such as therapy appointments, support groups, or wellness practices, that can help maintain stability and progress.

6. A crisis plan, including emergency contacts, local resources, and steps to take in case of a mental health emergency.

Sarah, in collaboration with her therapist, develops a detailed relapse prevention plan before concluding her course of CBT. She identifies her main triggers as relationship conflicts, work stress, and lack of sleep. Her warning signs include irritability, emotional reactivity, and urges to self-medicate with alcohol. To cope with these triggers, Sarah plans to use deep breathing and mindfulness exercises, as well as reaching out to her sister or best friend for support. She also makes a commitment to attending her weekly yoga class and monthly therapy check-ins, even when she's feeling good, to maintain her self-care routine. She creates a list of positive affirmations, such as "I am capable of handling difficult emotions" and "I deserve love and respect," to repeat to herself during challenging moments. Finally, she puts together a crisis plan, including the number for a local crisis hotline and the address of the nearest emergency room, in case her symptoms ever feel unmanageable.

It's important to note that a relapse prevention plan is not a guarantee against relapse, but rather a tool for reducing risk and increasing preparedness. Relapses can still happen, even with a solid plan in place. The key is to view relapses not as failures, but as opportunities for learning and growth. If a relapse does occur, it's important to respond with self-compassion and a recommitment to the strategies and supports outlined in the plan.

Michael, who has a history of impulsive behaviors and anger outbursts, experiences a relapse a few months after completing CBT. After receiving some critical feedback at work, he finds himself falling back into old patterns of rumination and self-criticism. Before he knows it, he's lashing out at his partner and contemplating quitting his job. However, because Michael has a relapse prevention plan in place, he's able to recognize these warning signs and take proactive steps to get back on track. He reaches out to his therapist for an extra session, practices his cognitive restructuring skills to challenge his negative thoughts, and takes a mental health day to engage in self-care activities. By catching the relapse early and responding with his predetermined coping strategies, Michael is able to prevent the situation from escalating and maintain his overall progress.

Relapse prevention planning should be an ongoing process, not a one-time event. As life circumstances and stressors change, the plan may need to be updated or adapted. Regular check-ins with oneself, as well as with a therapist or support network, can help identify any new triggers or warning signs, and ensure that coping strategies remain relevant and effective.

Emily, who has been in recovery from BPD for several years, makes a habit of reviewing and updating her relapse prevention plan every six months. At her most recent check-in, she realizes that some of her triggers have changed. With the recent loss of a family member, she's now more vulnerable to grief and loneliness. She adjusts her plan to include more social support and bereavement-specific coping strategies, such as attending a grief support group and journaling about her memories of her loved one. By staying proactive and adaptable in her planning, Emily is able to maintain her resilience and wellbeing, even in the face of significant life challenges.

Ultimately, the development of a comprehensive, individualized, and flexible relapse prevention plan is a powerful tool for maintaining the gains of CBT and promoting long-term recovery. By anticipating challenges, identifying personal triggers and warning signs, and having a concrete plan for coping and seeking support, individuals with BPD can reduce the risk of relapse and maintain their progress towards a life of stability, fulfillment, and resilience.

Establishing a support network and continuing self-care practices

A final key strategy for maintaining progress after CBT is the establishment of a robust support network and the continuation of regular self-care practices. Recovery from BPD is not a solo journey, and having a network of supportive, understanding individuals can make all the difference in navigating the ups and downs of the process. Similarly, engaging in consistent self-care practices can help promote emotional regulation, stress management, and overall well-being, all of which are crucial for sustaining the gains made in therapy.

A strong support network can include a variety of individuals, such as:

1. Family members and close friends who are understanding and reliable

2. Mental health professionals, such as a therapist or psychiatrist

3. Peer support specialists or sponsors, such as those found in 12-step programs or mental health support groups

4. Members of a faith community or spiritual group

5. Colleagues or classmates who are supportive and non-judgmental

When building a support network, it's important to choose individuals who are trustworthy, empathetic, and respectful of boundaries. Not everyone in an individual's life may be equipped to provide the kind of support needed, and that's okay. Quality is more important than quantity when it comes to support systems.

It can be helpful to have a range of supporters to turn to for different needs. For example, a close friend might be the go-to for a listening ear and a shoulder to cry on, while a therapist might be best for objective guidance and skills coaching. A peer support specialist might offer invaluable firsthand experience and encouragement, while a family member might provide practical help with daily tasks or responsibilities.

Sarah, who has a tendency to isolate when feeling depressed or anxious, makes a concerted effort to build and maintain her support network after completing CBT. She reaches out to a few close friends and family members, sharing her experiences in therapy and her goals for ongoing recovery. She asks for their support and sets clear expectations for what that might look like, such as regular check-ins, invitations to social activities, or help with household chores when she's feeling overwhelmed. Sarah also joins an online support group for individuals with BPD, where she can connect with others who understand her struggles and share coping strategies.

She continues to see her therapist once a month for maintenance sessions, and has the number of a crisis hotline saved in her phone for emergencies. By actively cultivating a diverse and reliable support system, Sarah feels more equipped to handle the challenges of recovery and less alone in her journey.

In addition to external support, ongoing self-care practices are crucial for maintaining mental and emotional wellbeing. Self-care refers to any intentional actions taken to care for one's physical, mental, and emotional health. This can look different for everyone, but some common self-care practices include:

1. Engaging in regular physical activity, such as walking, dancing, or playing sports

2. Practicing relaxation techniques, such as deep breathing, progressive muscle relaxation, or yoga

3. Pursuing creative hobbies, such as art, music, or writing

4. Spending time in nature, such as hiking, gardening, or stargazing

5. Nourishing the body with healthy foods and adequate hydration

6 Getting enough sleep and maintaining a consistent sleep schedule

7. Scheduling regular medical and dental check-ups

8. Engaging in activities that promote joy, laughter, and playfulness

9. Setting and maintaining healthy boundaries in relationships

10. Practicing self-compassion and positive self-talk

The key to effective self-care is finding activities that are enjoyable, sustainable, and promote a sense of balance and wellbeing. It's also important to prioritize self-care, even when life gets busy or stressful. Regular self-care can help prevent burnout, reduce stress, and increase resilience in the face of challenges.

Michael, who completed CBT over a year ago, has made self-care a non-negotiable part of his daily routine. He starts each morning with a 10-minute meditation practice, followed by a healthy breakfast and a brisk walk around his neighborhood. He's discovered a love for cooking, and makes a point to prepare nourishing meals for himself throughout the week. In the evenings, he winds down with a hot bath, a good book, and some gentle stretching. On weekends, he explores new hiking trails or tries out a new art class. By building self-care into his schedule and treating it as a priority, Michael finds that he's better able to manage stress, regulate his emotions, and maintain a positive outlook, even when faced with triggers or challenges.

It's worth noting that self-care is not a panacea, and it's not always easy to maintain, especially during times of high stress or symptom exacerbation. There may be times when an individual's usual self-care practices feel impossible or ineffective, and additional support is needed. This is where having a solid support network and relapse prevention plan can be especially vital.

Emily, who has been in recovery from BPD for several years, recently experienced a significant loss and found herself slipping back into old patterns of negative thinking and emotional dysregulation. Her usual self-care practices of journaling and yoga felt inadequate in the face of her grief, and she found herself isolating and neglecting her physical health. Recognizing these warning signs, Emily reached out to her therapist and attended a few extra sessions to process her emotions and adjust her coping strategies. She also leaned on her support group for encouragement and accountability, attending meetings even when she didn't feel like it.

Establishing a strong support network and engaging in regular self-care practices are not one-time events, but ongoing processes that require intentional effort and commitment. As life circumstances change and new challenges arise, individuals in recovery from BPD may need to reassess and adjust their support systems and self-care strategies to ensure they remain effective and relevant.

This might involve reaching out to new sources of support, such as a specialized therapy group or a mentor in a particular field of interest. It might also involve trying out new self-care activities, such as a mindfulness app or a creative writing class, to keep things fresh and engaging.

The key is to approach the maintenance of support and self-care with a spirit of curiosity, flexibility, and self-compassion. There is no one-size-fits-all formula for recovery, and what works for one person may not work for another. By staying open to new possibilities, being willing to adapt and adjust as needed, and treating oneself with kindness and understanding throughout the process, individuals with BPD can build a strong foundation for long-term success and wellbeing.

Ultimately, the journey of recovery from BPD is a deeply personal and ongoing one, requiring a commitment to self-discovery, skill-building, and self-care that extends far beyond the confines of a therapy room. By establishing a robust support network, engaging in regular self-care practices, and developing a comprehensive relapse prevention plan, individuals who have completed CBT can continue to build on their progress and thrive in their lives.

This is not to say that the journey will be easy or linear. There will undoubtedly be setbacks, challenges, and moments of doubt along the way. Recovery is rarely a straight line, and it's normal and expected to have ups and downs.

What matters most is how individuals respond to these challenges - with self-compassion, resilience, and a commitment to getting back on track. By viewing setbacks as opportunities for learning and growth, rather than as failures or evidence of personal deficiency, individuals in recovery can maintain a sense of hope and forward momentum, even in the face of adversity.

In the end, the goal of CBT for BPD is not just symptom reduction or behavioral change, but a fundamental shift in how individuals relate to themselves, others, and the world around them. It's about developing a new way of being - one characterized by self-awareness, self-acceptance, and self-directedness.

The skills and strategies learned in CBT provide a powerful toolkit for this transformation, but the real work of recovery happens in the day-to-day choices, habits, and perspectives that individuals cultivate over time. It's in the moments of choosing self-care over self-destruction, reaching out for help over isolating, and challenging negative thoughts over believing them.

By committing to this ongoing work of personal growth and self-discovery, individuals who have completed CBT for BPD can not only maintain their progress, but continue to expand their capacity for joy, connection, and fulfillment in all areas of their lives.

This is the true promise of recovery - not a life without challenges or pain, but a life in which challenges and pain can be met with resilience, wisdom, and grace. A life in which individuals are empowered to be the authors of their own stories, and to craft a narrative of healing, growth, and hope.

As we conclude this exploration of maintaining progress and preventing relapse after CBT for BPD, it's important to remember that this is not the end of the journey, but the beginning of a new chapter. A chapter that each individual has the power to write, one day and one choice at a time.

May all those who embark on this path find the strength, support, and self-compassion needed to thrive, and may they always remember that they are worthy of a life filled with love, meaning, and joy. The road ahead may be uncertain, but with the tools of CBT, the support of others, and the unwavering belief in one's own resilience, anything is possible.

www.ingramcontent.com/pod-product-compliance
Lightning Source LLC
Chambersburg PA
CBHW050819250726
48653CB00006B/2309